I INVENTED THE GAP YEAR

Paul W. King

For Zsa Zsa

PROLOGUE

I was euphoric, invincible, transformed. Forever changed. Deliriously high on the most exhilarating drug – dopamine.

Beguiled and enchanted by Mitsuko, a woman of exotic beauty and supreme femininity. The vision of her gentle smile and the warmth of her touch would remain with me forever, guarded safely in the treasure chest of my most prized memories.

She was remarkable, unique and very special. How lucky I had been to be with her - even if only for one night.

Now literally and metaphorically in another world, this initiation had evaporated the pall of guilt. My thoughts spinning, I stumbled down the stairs, along the corridor to my room and fell onto my bed. Instinctively I knew that experience had been a key part of the journey I was on.

Exhausted, in a surreal, dream-like state, I fell into fitful bouts of delirious sleep. During the semi-conscious moments my thoughts turned to where I was and how I had arrived here. I marvelled at my multi-dimensional travels which far exceeded the simple constraints of distance and time.

Reflecting not only on the journey that had brought me to Tokyo but more significantly to this juncture in my life. My home and parents on the other side of the world seemed so distant. Yet physical distance made no practical difference as I had always considered myself to be a peripheral member of the family, bound by it yet not an integral part of it.

My parents' life had been so orderly and predictable that despite not having seen or spoken to them for many months, I knew exactly what they would have been doing if they had been at home.

Was it to escape the boredom of routine and sameness that caused me to seek out adventure and excitement? Or is there some innate need in every young man to test himself, to demonstrate his warrior skills; to validate himself before returning home triumphantly to claim the respect of his elders?

BOOK 1

Chapter 1

STARTING OUT

Growing up in small-town England with 1950s post-war rationing and austerity I merely accepted the physical beauty that surrounded me and the stifling, restrictive nature of my home life. The former was provided by the idyllic setting of Seavale, the West Country seaside town in which we lived.

The latter was created in part by what I would later come to see as parents who had not found a formula for comfortable marriage and for whom the joys of happy family life remained elusive.

My parents presented themselves as being open-minded and liberal. They told me on numerous occasions I was free and in no way inhibited by life in the rectory. But, there were a few rules by which I had to abide. I was not allowed to go to the local cinema because in their opinion, the establishment was frequented by the wrong kind of people, and in any case there were no films worth watching.

The very fact that my parents disapproved of the cinema added to its allure. There were a few times when thinking my absence would not be noticed, I sneaked into the Curzon. I loved its overly-ornate Grecian decor interior, its red velour seats and felt the surge of excitement as people gathered. Quite different to the orderly, respectable way in which people arrived for a church service.

Yes, people were boisterous as they entered the cinema but they were there to have fun and enjoy themselves. Boys like me purchased one shilling tickets which put us right at the front, staring up at the screen. The middle rows of the cinema were often empty but the back rows were used by young couples.

They engaged in a regular and accepted ritual. The boy would at some stage pluck up sufficient courage to slide his arm round the girl. Then, with more courage and a bit of luck they would start to kiss.

A school friend had his very own radio. That was what I yearned for and finally obtained when I was 13 or 14. The pre-war dull-finish Bakelite box was more than compensated for by the hypnotic way its miracle producing thermionic valves glowed through the rear vents.

Moving the tuning dial allowed me to travel - to escape. Strange languages and all manner of exotic Eastern music poured out, swirling around my bedroom, transporting me to places of excitement. Even the fading in-and-out of the signal re-affirmed this sense of distance and ephemerality.

I was discouraged from talking with, let alone mixing with local youths who clearly did not fall into the category of middle-class. I was not allowed to raise my voice or display any form of rowdy behaviour. In my emotionally celibate family such feelings were considered inappropriate and therefore not to be displayed.

Apart from mandatory attendance at far too many church services, there was also an unremitting requirement to behave in an exemplary way. Periodic reminders reiterated that my father was rector and as such held a position within the community. His probity and rectitude were not to be sullied by my inappropriate behaviour.

But perfection does not come easily or naturally to young boys whose inclinations are to seek adventure and push the boundaries.

I have no doubt my father loved me. He did show affection within the non-demonstrative bounds of what he considered to be normal and socially acceptable. At times, he even permitted himself a fleeting sense of playfulness.

The predominant feeling was, however, of a man living in a separate world, encapsulated in, even imprisoned by his choice of profession. Secluded in his study most of the time, he appeared inordinately burdened with the social and financial responsibilities of his flock and family.

My mother suffered from pride, a common and harmless enough condition in many people, but in her case it was every bit as debilitating as a physical impairment. To compensate she contrived the image she wished to portray; that of upper-class superiority and confidence.

The reality was an emotionally brittle woman whose life had been blighted by the painfully restrictive class structure of the 1930s. It had created in her a need to display her apparent self-assurance so assertively it included denying her own children any opinions other than those which she herself espoused.

Not for her Voltaire's concept of tolerance, in which he said, 'I disapprove of what you say but will defend to the death your right to say it.'

At my all-boys school I was part of a group whose

common denominator was that none of us excelled at anything. The exception was my best friend Tony who did well in school and with whom I had never-ending discussions about girls.

The rest of my group congregated regularly at Mike's house because his permanently unseen psychiatrist father and anorexic mother were unusually open and liberal. Not only did they allow us to fill the living room with smoke from cheap Woodbine cigarettes but Mike talked uninhibitedly about how often his parents had sex.

'They are always at it,' was his proud boast. 'They make so much noise bouncing around on the bed and then come down laughing.'

How different to my parents who slept quietly in separate beds. Once I bravely asked my mother why they did not have a double bed like all my friends' parents. The response was that when they lived in India it was too hot and unhygienic to share a bed and so they had just carried on this practice after returning to England. A plausible explanation of circumstances which conveniently avoided any physical contact.

It was only on reflection that I realised my parents rarely touched each other. A dutiful, unemotional peck on the cheek at Christmas was about as passionate as I had ever seen them.

As a teenager on a camping trip in Europe the whole family witnessed an Italian father sweep up his little son, hug him lovingly and smother the curly-haired boy with kisses.

My parents recoiled in horror, their faces contorted at such unseemly behaviour. 'Disgusting' muttered my mother, and having been conditioned to emotional sobriety, I nodded in agreement.

In January 1960 the entire nation learnt a new word. 'Unexpurgated,' which in turn, inappropriately became synonymous with smut. It was the year of publication of the unexpurgated edition of D.H. Lawrence's novel, Lady Chatterley's Lover. A bold attempt by the publisher, Penguin, to circumvent the heavy armour of the British State's oppressive obscenity laws.

200,000 copies were sold on the first day of release and by the end of the year over 2 million copies had been sold - far outstripping sales of the usual best-seller, the Bible.

There were occasions at my school when the headmaster wished to address all pupils and staff about "something significant." The gravity and theatre of these pronouncements were apparent when everyone was summoned to congregate in the quadrangle.

The teachers, all of whom were male, wore academic gowns which fluttered in the breeze. They marshalled the boys, sometimes shouting out individual names - always surnames of course - to stop them talking or to move them into place.

The headmaster was an imposing figure, tall and physically robust. When still only in his mid-30s at the end of the war, he had reached the rank of Colonel. On this occasion there was the added gravitas of his crimson academic stole trimmed with white ermine (or vermin as we called it) denoting his Cambridge degree.

Standing high on the chapel steps he shouted, 'Whelby minor,' at the younger of the two Whelby brothers, 'stop jostling.' No threat of any particular punishment was required. When the headmaster spoke you obeyed. The feeling was that if God was at the top of the pyramid, the headmaster was not far below him.

He began his interdiction by saying, 'No doubt

everyone present is aware of the furore surrounding the recent court ruling relating to the publication of "Lady Chatterley's Lover".

'No one,' he said before pausing to cast his eye over the group. 'No one is to bring a copy of "that book" into this school. I cannot make myself any clearer than this - so take heed.'

Most people reading this book were unaware that the story was about the coming together of two vulnerable, isolated and lonely people. The population at large was purchasing a literary masterpiece solely to scavenge its sexually descriptive content.

It must have been obvious that within the apparently sophisticated Western world, there was huge pent-up frustration. A yearning to demystify sex and the need to enjoy and normalise human sexuality.

The poet Philip Larkin famously summed it up when he wrote to the effect that sex was invented in 1963 which was disappointingly, too late for him.

At school my best friend Tony and I held long conversations which skipped between youthful laughter and intensity. The recurring theme was always girls and the mysteries of sex. In the 1950s sex was indeed a mystery to everyone except Mike's parents. A time at which naming a West End musical show "The Pyjama Game" was considered mildly salacious and risqué.

Well over half a century ago, long before the age of the Internet, getting any information about sex was extremely difficult. The church, the legal system and adults in general paternalistically thought they were in some way safeguarding society and especially the young by keeping them in ignorance.

An example was James Douglas, editor of the

Sunday Express who said he would 'rather give young people a phial of prussic acid than let them read Radclyffe Hall's book "The Well of Loneliness"' chronicling a lesbian relationship.

School biology classes, the recognised form of reproductive (meaning sex) education at the time, were pretty useless. Frogs' cloacae just didn't seem to be that relevant or interesting.

On a visit to London at the age of fifteen I crossed the city, still pock-marked with bomb sites, to find a bookshop which a school-friend advised sold one or two books containing information about sex. Self-conscious, flustered and feeling intensely guilty I entered the shop and eventually found a slim volume with the word sex in the title. Flushed with embarrassment and without delay I paid the five shillings and fled.

For me this was as significant as finding the Holy Grail. I now thought I had in my possession a magical key to understanding the forbidden and unknown.

Eventually in the secrecy of my bedroom I furtively studied the book and did find some things of use. The clitoris was shown in my Charing Cross book but there was insufficient information about it to generate any interest. It appeared to be a small appendage with no greater significance than an earlobe. Certainly no mention of the fact that it contains twice as many nerve endings as the penis.

Taking the book to show Tony it did cross my mind that it would probably not be good news if I was caught with it at school. If you could be expelled for having Lady Chatterley's Lover what would they do if they caught me with this book? Hang, draw and quarter me?

At the age of sixteen I had an enchanting girlfriend. She was incredibly beautiful, with an adorable face, long blonde hair and lovely youthful figure. Everywhere we went, people looked at Claire. It was obvious that other boys and even older men could not take their eyes off her. What I did not understand at the time was that people not only looked at Claire but coveted our relationship, seeing us as a beautiful and enviable young couple.

Three years before the publication of Helen Gurley Brown's book "Sex and the Single Girl" premarital sex was still theoretically considered inappropriate.

At a time when most people were church-goers, the prevailing social norms pretended that nice girls just simply did not engage in premarital sex beyond a little petting.

Having said that, the formalising of a relationship with time or by betrothal frequently made premarital sex more acceptable. Men usually didn't care, but some women managed a series of 'unofficial engagements' which provided a lifestyle marginally closer to that of today.

Lynne Reid Banks 1960 novel "The L-Shaped Room" in its 1962 film version, realistically and painfully show the prevailing moral attitudes of the time. The appalling social stigma of being an unmarried mother.

Opprobrium at the concept of a 27-year- old virgin who has joyless sex with a man who then denounces her simply because she had allowed him to have sex with her. Then after enjoying sex within a mutually loving relationship, a second man (and it would appear society in general) considered her to be no better than a prostitute.

As a boy I do not remember my parents ever mentioning sex directly. Occasionally in their awkward, prudish way they might make a disapproving reference to someone having "an affair". Obliquely, my mother made it apparent that in her opinion sex was a pretty unpleasant business inflicted on women by men.

If only I had been lucky enough to have had the experience of Tony Wedgewood-Benn who was quoted as saying, "When I asked my mother about sex, she said, 'Darling, it's so beautiful I can't tell you about it.'"

In the year and a half we were together, Claire only visited the rectory two or three times. While not rude, my parents never extended a warm welcome. Even the house itself probably felt chilly to her. It was an imposing Edwardian structure set in large grounds in the best part of the town.

Like all rectories and vicarages, it was owned by the Church of England who rarely undertook any maintenance. The result being that any sense of affluence was quickly negated by its shabby appearance, chipped paint and unkempt garden.

'Come into the drawing-room,' commanded my mother, doing her Lady Bracknell routine. Still in full "Am-Dram" acting mode she imperiously said 'Sit here,' pointing to a well-worn armchair some distance from the large sofa on which we could comfortably have sat together.

A few minutes later as she passed my father in the hall, we overheard her muttering 'He's far too young for that kind of thing.' Knowing my mother, it is probable that we were intended to hear that remark.

My parents may have thought having a girlfriend was a distraction from schoolwork. In reality, I found it difficult to flourish in the classroom. I languished near the bottom of my set in a permanent state of cortisol-producing anxiety, always fearful of the next public revelation of my dimwittedness.

One teacher at my prep-school who appeared to take pleasure in repeatedly highlighting my inadequacies was a Church of England priest. It made no sense to me that this man could preach about the qualities of kindness and mercy while at the same time taking obvious amusement in humiliating me in front of the class about my poor spelling.

This incident and other observations of hypocrisy and duplicity by church members caused me to start questioning the very nature of religious belief. What people espoused and how they acted often differed.

Along those lines, I could not understand why God had to be so obscure. Why couldn't he be visible and accessible to all, thus avoiding all the doubt and confusion?

I really tried to work hard at school but regardless of the amount of effort I put in I just could not remember things such as multiplication tables and, despite loving history could not remember dates. Worst of all was that strange assemblage of numbers, letters and brackets called algebra, which fortunately I was never to encounter again after leaving school.

I was considered by my teachers to be a bit "dim". A disparaging and demoralising sentiment shared by my parents long before anyone had heard of, let alone recognised or acknowledged a condition called dyslexia. At seventeen I was trapped by a debilitating sense of shame, burdened with a self-perception of incompetence and the prospect of never achieving anything worthwhile in life.

Unsaid but apparent to me, my somewhat scholarly father was disappointed that his younger son would never be entering one of the professions. My mother was equally disappointed because she was unable to recognise anything in me which reflected appropriately well on her.

Although not strictly true, I was told that there would be no opportunities for me in our small town and I was required to move away immediately after leaving school. This produced mixed feelings; I did want to escape my repressive home life but there was also an element of severity in forcing me out with no discussion or the provision of options.

The net result was that I became totally self-supporting financially and, more significantly emotionally, from my eighteenth birthday onwards.

During this post-war period of reconstruction fewer than four per cent of school leavers went to university and substantially less than fifty per cent of MPs were graduates. So comparatively uncommon was university attendance at this time that those who did go to such institutions, had their names proudly painted on the school's scholarship board.

Even in this time of lower emphasis on academic qualifications I was surprisingly offered jobs by four different companies. All of the jobs were that of a "management trainee" which at the time, was a recognised form of business apprenticeship; a sort of industrial midshipman.

I had been anxious to work overseas or at least find a job with the potential to take me overseas. This came from my belief that from the eighteenth-century onwards young men with drive but no family connections or money, could progress further and faster in the distant corners of the British Empire.

My parents were part of the last generation which had fanned out to the colonies as administrators and traders. They were married in India and both my brother and I were born there.

On many occasions I visited the homes of elderly people and was fascinated by the assorted treasures they had acquired during periods of colonial service.

Assegai spears, Maasai shields, huge brass shell casings made into walking-stick stands, tiger skins and copious quantities of carved ivory. Solid silver trophies with worthy inscriptions from once significant institutions such as the Kano Cricketers or the Darjeeling Racquets Club.

As a boy of about eight, I had been to a friend's large Victorian house. There was something special in the attic he wanted to show me. In the semi-darkness we opened a large case and took out an extremely long, heavy rifle.

I had seen .303s in war films but this gun and ammunition seemed very much larger. We played with the gun, pushing enormous cartridges into the chamber before trying to throw forward the bolt which fortunately, we did not have the strength to lock. 'My grandfather calls this his elephant gun,' the friend said proudly.

On a much grander scale the Marquess of Curzon had installed many of his hunting trophies together with his mistress (novelist Elinor Glyn) in one of his mansions, Montacute House. This led to the rhyme:

'Would you like to sin with Elinor Glyn
on a tiger skin?
Or would you prefer to err, with her,
on another fur?

The post-war era saw many former colonies gaining independence. But for me there was still glamour attached to working overseas as described in Somerset Maugham's emotional stories, set in mysterious and romantic sounding places like Borneo and the Federated Malay States.

The revelations of impetuous behaviour and its resultant turmoil, born out of and set against, jungle backdrops of stultifying heat, isolation and loneliness. Tales of transgression; people erupting self-destructively out of their stagnant lives.

Two of the jobs I was offered would have taken me directly overseas. I could have joined one company as a tea-planter in Assam. The other would have moved me to the goldmines of Sierra Leone.

The tea-planting job required five lonely, isolated years before a paid sea-passage and home-leave would be available. The gold-mining job was similar, but anyway West Africa did not hold the same appeal as Asia. By today's standards, sending a boy who had not yet turned eighteen to such places seems both remarkable and Dickensian.

Of the two jobs in England, I chose to work for a food-manufacturing company based twenty miles west of London. This choice was partly based on the knowledge that lodgings were available in the vicinity.

Although quite large, employing over 500 people, this was a family-owned business with its chairman Sir John supported by his fellow old Etonian nephew, as Managing Director. The other management trainees and junior managers, none of whom had been to university, all came from third-tier public schools.

Schools like Haileybury Imperial Service College and Ardingly College which had been established in the Victorian era to produce managers and soldiers who would be efficient and useful servants of the British Empire. The sort of chilblain-inducing schools E.M.Forster described as 'producing young men with well-developed bodies, fairly developed minds and undeveloped hearts.'

'What's your name and which school did you go to?' was how I remember being greeted by one arrogant little prick when I first joined the management trainee table in the staff dining room. The question had about as much refinement and subtlety as one dog smelling the butt of another.

Which school the trainee had attended contributed to the social hierarchy and corporate pecking order. Dressing impeccably in suits, usually three-piece suits was de rigueur, as was speaking with the right accent.

The French writer and philosopher Voltaire said of the British class system, 'The people are like their own beer, froth on top, dregs at the bottom, but the middle is excellent.'

Two hundred years later the British classes were still theoretically lumped into three categories. This belied the reality that there was an infinite gradation of class between those who laboured manually and the pedigreed, land-owning aristocracy.

How someone spoke could slide them up or down a notch or two on this scale. The stentorian, eternally upbeat voice of Pathé newsreader Bob Danvers-Walker authoritatively set the standard for upper-middle class speech.

All such accents now seem pretentious and anachronistic when heard on vintage film. No-one says orf for off, and other than South Africans, no-one refers to their black cat as a bleck ket. Even the Queen has modified her speech over the years and no longer uses the precious and rarefied accent she had at the time of her coronation.

Vera Lynn the singer who became the "Forces Sweetheart" during the war had been born in East Ham and originally spoke with a local London accent. Yet when interviewed in 1947 she had noticeably acquired the BBC standard RP (received pronunciation) accent. The same "acceptable" accent pressed upon all young actors at Rada.

Adding to the requirement to speak appropriately the social minefield was further complicated by which word was used for the same thing. Using the word toilet was plebeian and wholly unacceptable, as was referring to a serviette. The middle-class and above would all refer to the lavatory and napkins.

Most telling of all was the word used for the midday meal. Middle-class and above would always refer to it as lunch, or even luncheon, while others referred to it as dinner.

In addition to three-piece suits, young men aspiring to gentility wore a signet ring on the little finger of the left-hand. Ideally this should be of plain gold but occasionally it could be in inlaid with a simple stone, so long as it was no more garish than Black Onyx.

Having initials engraved on this ring would be as great a faux-pas as using the word toilet. The correct thing was to have the signet ring deeply, reverse-engraved with a crest which in turn could be used as an old-fashioned wax seal.

Reminiscent of "Tess of the d'Urbervilles," those without legitimate entitlement to a family coat of arms would find a distant or dubious connection to nobility. So it was with me, taking great pride in the specious status conferred by the intaglio gold signet ring I received as an eighteenth birthday present.

The first time I returned home after an absence of four months was for the Christmas holiday. I had spent the equivalent of two weeks' salary to purchase a carefully selected gift for Claire and was desperate to see her.

She told me she had been on a few dates. Because I was going away we had released each other to give both of us exactly that freedom. A freedom which had obviously been employed more successfully by Claire than by me. She was now more passionate and it was apparent that she had been tutored by someone with greater expertise than mine.

She asked if I was seeing anyone. Caught off-guard and thinking our relationship was over, I lied, and face-savingly boasted I was dating a model. Perhaps if I'd just been honest and told her how much I wanted her... This distant, faded memory of teenage love and ineptitude still lingers. Had I been gallant or foolish, sensible or stupid in how I handled my relationship with Claire? Though you cannot superimpose the values of one generation on another, and by definition cannot give the wisdom of maturity to the young.

I consoled myself thinking optimistically of the comment Mrs. Nicholson, the observant and sensitive doctor's wife made sometime later. Although she had children of her own I was able to confide in her, in a way that I could not speak to anyone else.

It was she who said, 'Women always remember fondly the man whom they first loved. Similar affection may or may not be awarded to the man with whom they first made love.

We all have a first love, a last love and usually some in between. Perhaps it is worth remembering the invocation that "we should love everyone who is worthy of being loved." 'However,' she continued, 'we have to bear in mind that if we are free to share our love with other people, then so too are they.'

At the time of my first job, with no television to

distract, I did read a few books such as Bonjour Tristesse. Sitting on the bed in my damp, gloomy room it seemed incomprehensible to me that this book about such decadent lifestyles had been written by an eighteen year-old French girl. (Françoise Sagan)

How on earth could she be so worldly? (To which part of the answer would have been that she did not have the misfortune to grow up in a rectory.)

Also on my reading list were stories by imaginative writers such as Guy de Maupassant. He would attend funerals, weddings and other gatherings simply to observe people's interaction. It was he who said, 'Where emotion is, there am I.'

The emotional turmoil pervading peoples' lives in de Maupassant's stories carried me away. If there was a universal theme, it was that all the protagonists had transgressed. Pursuing some obsession they had broken out of their constraints and deviated from the norms of their society; in turn paying a heavy price for doing so.

I definitely wanted the excitement but was fearful about paying the heavy price. My parents' philosophy cautioned that a moment of glory or a moment of passion, was never worth a potential lifetime of pain and regret. What they failed to tell me or even to recognise themselves, was the necessity to take some risks in order to create a fulfilling life.

Making what was for me a major investment, I purchased a portable radio. Its primary purpose was to allow me to listen to pop music. The sort of music totally disapproved of by my parents and therefore never allowed in our house. What was acceptable to them was limited to classical music.

Popular music was going through a massive shift at

this time, yet groups like the Beatles and the Stones still wore jackets and ties. The "Golden Strings" of Mantovani's violins were being swept aside by steel string guitars and the glorious Appalachian harmony of the Everly Brothers.

The melancholic lyrics they sang seemed so relevant to me. The apparently endless search for love and happiness, yearned for to offset loneliness and emptiness.

And the titles of their songs such as "I'll Never Get Over You," "When Will I Be Loved?" "Don't Let Our Love Die," were so spot on with my teenage emotions.

Little Richard built on the musical tradition of high-paced, high-energy black gospel music which was literally shouted out. His outrageously flamboyant 1955 performance of "Tutti-Frutti" caused a seismic shift and gave birth to rock 'n' roll.

So shocking and scandalous was this music that it was universally damned by everyone: except of course teenagers. When I say universally damned that is what I mean. The middle classes in Europe and America considered it to be ridiculous, disgusting and grossly immoral.

Broadcasting in England was tightly controlled by the BBC a stalwart of the Establishment. So concerned were they with keeping up standards that announcers and panellists were required to wear dinner jackets not only on television but on radio as well.

In an attempt to protect their listeners from that which they deemed to be inappropriate they banned the broadcasting of great swathes of pop music. In response to this, "pirate" broadcasters, understanding the demand, set up crackly overseas stations such as Radio Luxembourg.

Even more bizarrely Radio Caroline operated from

a ship outside UK waters. The British government was so incensed by this, that in the Marine Offences Act of 1967, they made it illegal for a British subject to associate with Radio Caroline.

Following one of my Saturday morning pop sessions I heard a BBC radio programme which enthralled me and was to start a lifelong interest in human behaviour.

It was a talk given by the academic Dr. Fernando Henriques. This sociologist was remarkable because of his numerous, un-British references to sexual practises in a range of cultures.

It gave me my first faint sense that maybe I was not alone or abnormal in my preoccupation with sex. Although governed by different social and religious laws, interest in sex was universal and a significant part of human life.

In the library I was attracted to anything which would help me to learn about human interaction. One of the first books I read was, Freud's "Interpretation of Dreams." Not an easy book to follow but worthwhile because of the insights it gave me.

There had been a long tradition of "lodging" in which predominantly single men would live with a family or a widow. They would pay weekly rent in return for which they received board and lodging.

My modest lodgings were in a dilapidated, mid-terrace Victorian workers' house in the poorest part of town. There were two rooms upstairs, one of which I occupied and two rooms downstairs, one of which at the front was used as a bedroom by my landlady Mrs Granby, whom I called "G".

Tacked onto the rear of the house was a small, gloomy kitchen. It did not contain a refrigerator but as it was north-facing and permanently cold it did not need one. White chips on the large, rectangular earthenware sink contrasted with its overall, depressing olive-coloured glaze.

The oversized single cold-tap rattled and shook noisily as if complaining that like the rest of the house, it was too old and tired still to be working. Although having a tap was a step up from some people in rural areas who still had to pump water.

Similarly, over six million people used an outside lavatory. In my accommodation, the original outside lavatory was now accessible from the kitchen which presumably elevated the status of the house to one boasting "indoor plumbing".

Dangling from the high-mounted cistern was an ancient chain which had long since lost whatever handle had originally been attached to it. Moreover, it was definitely time to renew the flaking whitewash on the brick walls, but this like any other type of repair or renovation was never contemplated.

While none too pleased with this arrangement I could tolerate the coldness, the uneven red brick floor and the perpetually damp wooden seat. What did appal me were the hand-torn sheets of newspaper pressed onto a nail in the door. Even the tracing-paper-like toilet rolls provided in British Rail lavatories were preferable to this.

There was no bathroom; when I wanted a bath an old fashioned metal tub was taken down from the hook on which it hung on an outside wall. Placed on the kitchen floor it was filled to a depth of a few inches with hot water via a short length of tubing from the gas Ascot heater.

Prior to running the water it was necessary to put a few coins in the meter. After use, the tub was bailed out into the sink until the residue could be poured out of the back door.

During the winter, heavy curtains which hung from hinged metal arms in the living room were swung over to cover the doors to the kitchen and hallway. Roles of stuffed fabric referred to as sausages were placed along the bottom of the same two doors, keeping out the worst of the drafts.

In the coldest weather when frost formed on the inside of the window, the living room was heated for up to an hour with an oil-stove which, however, carefully it had been filled, always smelled of paraffin. If the wick had not been properly trimmed it emitted a visible plume of black smoke which over the years had darkened the ceiling.

My bed was made up with rectangular flannel sheets, heavy blankets and what was referred to as an eiderdown. A presumptuous name for an inexpensive substitute which was probably stuffed with chicken feathers. This in turn was covered by a candlewick bedspread, every movement of which produced a pollen-like bloom of white specks.

Annoyingly this lint stuck more tenaciously to my black suit than to the bed covering from which it had been spawned. On winter nights a "stone" (ceramic) hot water bottle was filled from the kettle. As there was no cover on this it had the capacity to burn feet and hands if not used with care.

The view from my small room at the rear of the house was of a narrow, weed-lined passageway with a dilapidated fence separating Mrs. G's property from the mirror-image house next door. I never got to know the neighbours but understood that they also were too poor to be house-proud.

Like G, they were working-class people who had been renting these properties for many years. Legislation had frozen the rents and given the tenants legal right to remain as long as they wished. Whoever the unseen landlords were, they had no interest in undertaking any repairs. They only wanted the tenants to die off so they could re-rent the properties for a better return.

I fully understood people who struggled financially. My salary was £450 per annum, which was paid monthly in cash in a small manila envelope. (The factory staff were paid weekly. Very weakly according to them.)

My salary equated to less than nine pounds per week from which there were deductions of about one and a half pounds. I had to pay my landlady three pounds ten-shillings a week after which there was not much left over with which to buy those all-important clothes, let alone pay for entertainment.

As in the vast majority of working-class homes there was no telephone. If I wanted to make a call, I walked to the traditional red telephone box outside the corner shop at the end of the street.

When making calls from these public phones it was necessary to insert three large copper pennies and then use the rotary dial to register the numbers. It seemed to take so long for the dial to return from the higher numbers. When someone responded, button "A" was pressed. If there was no answer, the caller pressed button "B" and the coins clattered noisily into the return dish.

Sometimes there would be someone on the phone and a couple of others waiting their turn. If the people waiting thought the user had been talking for too long they would tap loudly on the glass with their heavy coins.

Those people waiting outside the telephone box could hear every word said by the person inside. Particularly distressing for any shy and embarrassed young men, who trying to reach a girl they barely knew, first had to negotiate the minefield of whichever parent answered the phone.

Within six months of starting work, during which I had been rotated through a couple of departments, I was called into the sales-manager's office. He asked if I would like to take over a sales territory on a temporary basis.

Although I was asked, it was in fact an instruction, which in those days and in my position was to be obeyed. Without knowing it I was about to play a minor role in, and witness the sadness of another man's decline.

My instructions were to take the train to Reading and find the house of a company employee who would then give me sales registers and information about all the accounts to be visited. I arrived at the modest, 1930s semi-detached house at about 10.30 in the morning, crisply dressed in one of my old school shirts with its starched, detachable collar.

Mrs. G had kindly pressed my suit trousers the night before with the heavy old flat-iron she heated on a metal sheet over the gas stove. There were electric irons at that time but "G" had never adapted to them since her time "in service" in the early 1900s.

It surprised me to see Mr. Jones in an open-necked shirt and house-shoes. He greeted me kindly but I thought I detected a faint smell of whiskey mingled with peppermint. We sat at the kitchen table and looked through the business record books. Needing more space Mr. Jones pushed aside a dish still encrusted with the remains of a meal that had obviously been dispensed with sometime ago.

I could not understand how anybody could let

themselves deteriorate so badly. At the same time I felt sorry for this miserable, forlorn creature. A man who carried himself in a hunched way, visibly acknowledging to the world that his life had been worthless; a man resigned to remorseless decline.

Mr. Jones, who was probably about 50, looked much older, displaying the florid, craggy face and shaky hands of an alcoholic. He spoke with quite a good accent but his sentences were halting, sometimes incomplete, trailing off as if what he was saying really didn't matter. There was a woman's apron hanging in the kitchen and there were other signs of a woman's presence, but Mrs. Jones was obviously not there and no reference was made of her until Mr. Jones blurted out:

'You obviously know about my wife?' When I replied that I did not, tears welled up in his eyes. He said, 'It was three months ago. I had one of my bad nights and woke late. My wife, who always got up early, was still in bed beside me. She was dead.'

I gathered up the paperwork and Mr. Jones handed me the keys to the pale-green, company-owned Hillman Minx parked in the driveway. It never occurred to me that the company had used me to undertake a job no one else wanted to do. But the outcome was that a fresh young eighteen year-old had been sent to invade the privacy of Mr. Jones' home and deliver the coup de grâce.

The self-satisfied lesson I took from this meeting was the determination never to be controlled by a need for alcohol or any other drug.

It was only later that my youthful arrogance softened to pity and understanding when I learned the full story of Mr. Jones' long ordeal. The recurring nightmares from which he suffered took him back, night after night, to his time of imprisonment and the constant mental subjugation and irrational brutality meted out on the Burma railway.

To his time as a slave labourer enduring the ever-present threat of arbitrary decapitation by his Japanese guards.

Unusually for people of my age, I was genuinely aware of the debt my generation owed the previous one. I found the words of Laurence Binyon's 1914 poem, "For the Fallen" to be poignant and moving.

"They shall not grow old as we that are left grow old; Age shall not weary them, nor the years condemn. At the going down of the sun and in the morning; we will remember them."

Sermons at Remembrance Day services reiterated over and over again, that those who had died during the wars, and those who returned from them damaged in mind and body, had given so much in order to protect the freedoms which we now enjoyed.

Moreover, two of the boys in my year at school were "father-less" at a time when two-parent families were the norm. One boy's father had been a bomber pilot and the other boy refused to speak of his father, other than to confirm he had been killed during the war.

My self-consciousness and shyness were manifested in a variety of ways: I became tongue-tied and blushed easily. This stemmed from the feeling that the spotlight was always on me. To some extent it had been, in that my home life had been an ongoing review of my imperfections.

My lack of self-assurance was put to the test when I had to walk into numerous businesses, introduce myself, regurgitate a suitable explanation for Mr. Jones' absence and start doing business. Painful though this experience was it did become easier with practice and had the effect of building a level of confidence.

I had always been tall for my age, six-foot by fourteen. Now at about six foot two, everyone assumed I was older. The strict discipline of my home and school left an impression of dependability and steadfastness.

After a few weeks I was given another temporary sales assignment. This required moving to Lincolnshire where I set up base in a provincial hotel. The main advantages for me were that I had a company Hillman Minx and was now living on expenses. My board and lodging being paid for allowed me to accumulate a little money.

The commercial hotel which became my temporary home was typical of many in which I would stay during the coming year. The bedroom itself contained only a single bed with an ancient bedside table on which there was a low-wattage lamp. In such hotels there was usually only one bathroom and a separate lavatory on each floor. The guests, almost universally men, probably all peed into the washbasin in their room when the lavatory was occupied or when they could not be bothered to walk down the corridor.

There was a communal lounge in which guests sat in rows on upright chairs taken from the dining room, watching the small black and white television set, occasionally arguing over which of the two stations they should view. On retiring at night it was standard practice to leave a pair of leather shoes outside the unlocked bedroom door to be cleaned by the night porter.

Most men smoked in those days and every part of the shabby commercial hotel smelled of stale smoke, kitchen cabbage and mildew. In the Lincolnshire hotel there were two Irish girls working as combined waitresses and chamber maids. I was attracted to Mary and summoned up the courage to ask her out.

In that type of hotel, a wake-up call consisted of a knock at the door accompanied by a cup of tea. Who delivered that tea varied from hotel to hotel. Often it was the night porter, the same geriatric man whose job it was to clean all the shoes. But in the Lincolnshire hotel it was the two girls who knocked on doors, and after hearing the guest say 'come in', would enter with the tea, while leaving the door ajar.

On one occasion, parked in my car, Mary giggled and said, 'I don't know if I should tell you this... but when Ann delivered your tea for the first time she rushed back to the kitchen flush with excitement. She said you looked so beautiful with your lovely tousled hair on the pillow.'

From then on Mary made sure that it was she who delivered my tea. As soon as she had put the tea on the bedside table I would pull her onto the bed and kiss her. This was by necessity a fleeting and innocent enough encounter but it did add a little excitement for both of us at the start of our day.

Mary, who was probably about twenty asked me how old I was. When told I was eighteen she did not believe me. She found it inconceivable that someone my age could be as mature as me and in a job such as mine.

She told me she was not happy working in the hotel and planned to return to Ireland as soon as she had saved up enough money to make the journey.

A couple of weeks later, when it was time for me

to leave, I placed a five-pound note in the pocket of her coat which always hung in the hallway outside the kitchen. It was not in an envelope and there was no note. I did not wish to embarrass her by trying to give her money which I knew she would not accept.

The food company found my single status and reliability useful which in turn led to a continuation of short term assignments. The travel plans I submitted to the company always included the location of a post office where I would be at nine A.M. every day. This allowed me to collect 'poste restante' mail, including my all-important salary and expenses which arrived as cash in notes and coins. Of equal importance was that it identified a place where the district sales manager could find me.

I travelled extensively around the country building up both my confidence and my financial reserves. But there were unwelcome disadvantages to this lifestyle, foremost of which was my inability to make and sustain friendships. Having a car turned out to be paradoxical.

It was what I wanted and needed most in order to build my social life. Yet, being constantly on the move it was not possible to meet people and develop friendships.

There was the occasional date, but mostly as a result of my shyness, this was a lonely life. Without emotional support from anyone, the words of a Platters song seemed to sum up my situation exactly.

It referred to an isolated, needy person who concealed his loneliness by pretending to the outside world that everything in his life was going well.

At nineteen I had become the opposite of what I wanted to be. Instead of being gregarious I had become solitory. I wanted a girlfriend and should have had one. I wanted to be with someone with whom I could act my age, have fun and be sexual.

My loneliness was exacerbated by the underlying feeling that I had been shunted out of home. My mother made no secret of the fact that she was pleased to be rid of me. Although never direct in her communication she did not hide the fact that her life would improve without the burden of this moody teenager.

My father, to his credit as a husband, always backed and supported my mother. As a boy, there were a few occasions when some, now long-forgotten transgression so incensed my mother she insisted my father should cane me. Kneeling over the bed he used a bamboo switch kept specifically for that purpose, but I always sensed my father really wanted no part of it.

It felt as though there was no-one who really cared about me. I believed that my failure extended beyond the classroom and included my inability to socialise normally within or outside my family. Was I destined forever to continue my litany of failure?

Even within the narrow band of the company's salesman there was a class structure. Top-class food emporia such as Fortnum and Mason or Harrods were visited by a rather pretentious little man, who retaining his wartime army rank, always introduced himself as Captain Farrar.

At the other end of the scale, the transport cafes around Birmingham were called on by a former naval rating. Harold or 'Arold as he pronounced it, had not been on a ship for a decade but he still walked with a peculiar rolling gait.

It was while on assignment with Harold in the Midlands that I was taken to a working-men's club. For someone desperate to elevate his social status this was clearly a step in the wrong direction. The room itself was totally unappealing, the brown anaglypta wallpaper further darkened by years of nicotine staining.

The wooden floorboards had a thin covering of absorbent sawdust which was in need of being changed. I was actually relieved to be with Harold who acted as a sort of buffer between me and the army of incoherent manual labourers. Most of these "union" men worked in the nearby coal mine or steel mill. Given the nature of their hot dusty work it was understandable that they developed a routine of drinking beer in the evenings.

The beer was inexpensive because the clubs had learned a trick from London "gentlemen's clubs." By forming a private entity they were able to avoid some licensing laws and brewery monopolies.

For entertainment there was a rather embarrassing comedian who battled on stoically regardless of the indifference displayed by his audience. Then a female singer came on. She was talented, refined, polished and startlingly beautiful. Some of the boorish miners and steelworkers quietened down to listen, but not everyone.

There were a couple of tables of inebriated men who, in their incomprehensible accents appeared to be competing to shout out the crudest and most suggestive remarks.

Slightly woozy with beer I could not take my eyes off this beautiful woman. I was nevertheless aware of a seedy, older-looking man who was obviously with her. Was he her husband, lover, agent or minder? It seemed so unfair and inappropriate that such a jewel should be in the control of this man. Especially as I would gladly and gallantly have been available to provide any services she might have required.

Despite my urgency to get on with life I started to

recognise that in every profession you had to start at the bottom and work your way up. That out of necessity we all have to compromise: we are all in the grip of people and circumstances that would not be of our choosing.

Chapter 2

POWIDSKY

I knew I did not wish to stay in this job although there were long-term prospects of working in one of the overseas offices. Like many young men, I wanted to move ahead far too quickly.

Just after my 19th birthday, I saw a newspaper advertisement from a man who planned to sail around the world and was looking for a young crew member who would contribute £500.

Isolated and bored I escaped in opiate-like daydreams of excitement and adventure. Picturing myself as macho, rugged and weather-beaten. Wearing shorts and a muscle revealing denim cut-off jacket, stepping ashore onto the soft, warm sand of a Caribbean beach.

I had an overwhelming urge to break out of the conventional mould into which I had been cast and reinvent myself as a risk-taker and adventurer. I wanted to write something meaningful on the blank sheet of my life but had no idea what.

Having replied to the advertisement I received the following neatly handwritten letter.

Address   T. K. Powidski   Q.M.
6 Windor Terrace, The Hoe
Plymouth, Devon
Polish home number
tel, 65933

13.9.62

Dear Sir,

Receiving your letter today, I reply immediately. It seems that the old spirit of adventure, the pioneering spirit of Plymouthians died with comfort and civilisation. Yours was the only reply to my ad.

Sincerely, I would not even consider your offer, except that I want to sail out this year. Your £200 and mine £100 cash in hand, will force us, if we come to an agreement, to cut down the provisions, medical kit and other items to the bare essentials.

Anyway if it is possible, would be better if you came to Plymouth, to meet me, see the boat, (In which I have invested more than £1000 already) hear my plans and judge yourself.

I don't want to discourage you, not knowing your disposition toward foreigners, but I am a Pole, 54 years, strong and healthy, feeling 35. Very good education and family, speaking eight languages, ex-artillery officer, now experienced seamen.

Awaiting your kind reply, the phone call or personal appearance.

I sent sincere greetings yours faithfully,
T.K. Powidski

This letter both excited and scared me. Surely this would prove to be the most amazing adventure? Sailing a small boat across the Atlantic and possibly around the world, landing in strange ports and living a totally different life. Equally, the reference to having minimal supplies and no prospect of earning any money did not seem very practical.

I phoned Powidski but had considerable difficulty understanding his accent. Acknowledging my age and insecurity, I returned to the rectory to discuss the matter.

As customary, I knocked on the door of my father's book-lined study and asked if I could talk to him. My father moved from his usual position behind the desk to one of the less formal chairs.

He listened without commenting and carefully read the letter. 'It does sound very exciting' he said. 'But you really would want to learn a lot more about the seaworthiness of the boat and the character of the man with whom you would be in such close confinement for so long.'

The first point resonated with me. Living in a seaside town I was well aware the sea could be beautiful and benign but also turbulent and terrifying. I had experienced the violence of winter storms, albeit from the safety of shore.

Three or four times each year, usually in the cold darkness of a mid-winter night, I heard the wailing siren-call for the lifeboat-men to jump into action. Aware that I was safe in bed, I imagined the brave crew as their lifeboat pitched and yawed through heavy seas towards a stricken vessel.

My father was calm and understanding. He made no attempt to forbid me from undertaking the voyage, although perhaps surprisingly to both of us, I would have obeyed had he done so. Instead my father gently guided me saying, 'You might want to think about what other options you have. Is there anything else you would like to do that is less dangerous?

After a few days consideration I wrote to Powidski acknowledging the courtesy of his letter but saying that I would not be proceeding.

His reply of September 20, 1962 was:

Dear Friend,
Thank you for your letter, never mind your refusal. It will be much better next year. I will be ready to go anyway if I find someone else or if you resolve to go next year, we will have spare cash.

I am still in Plymouth for a few days. Then I shall go to London, Liverpool or Southampton, because I can sit here all year and not a hope for a decent job.

Save your money, exercise and harden your guts, as you say, you will need them.

All best wishes, from your friend

Tadeusz

As thoughts of sailing around the world faded, my brother and I took advantage of a new type of holiday. For thirty-five guineas, it was possible to get a one-week holiday in a Spanish beach resort.

The whole idea of buying a holiday as a package, which included transportation, food and accommodation, was comparatively new. In an age when the vast majority of people had never been in an aeroplane there was the added excitement and trepidation of a flight.

My older brother James had been four academic years ahead of me and we had never attended the same school at the same time. He had been both scholarly and a competent sportsman, winning a commendable number of prizes and trophies. I was only 13 turning 14 when James left home to start a full-time job in the industrial midlands, training to be an engineer.

We did subsequently overlap at times, such as Christmas, but the reality was we did not know each other very well. This did not stop me from idolising him, envying his dark hair which I considered to be more masculine than my own effeminate, fair colouring.

As a boy I had on occasion used burnt matches to darken my eyebrows and would plaster my hair with Brylcreem in an attempt to control the waves and tone down my blondness.

In the Spanish resort hotel we met two sisters and quickly became a foursome. We had fun and considered ourselves very worldly as we savoured the fishy aroma of paella and choked on streams of wine from a porron.

In the warm sunshine I and the blonde sister Beth, started a teenage romance. More out of wishful thinking than any real sense of expectation, I had come suitably prepared with a few Durex. Now, somewhat to my surprise I was able to put them to use.

Every beach bar, cafe and nightclub, in fact everywhere we went, we heard a slow, romantically dreamy piece of guitar music called Maria Elena. As it formed a backdrop to everything we did, we thought of it as 'our' piece of music.

Towards the end of the week, Beth told me that the condoms were unnecessary because she was on the recently developed contraceptive pill. This threw me somewhat as I knew that no GP would ever prescribe the pill to an unmarried woman.

'I went to the Mary Stopes clinic in London. The only place where someone like me would be given a prescription,' Beth said. But I remained uncomfortable with the whole idea. For a young, unmarried woman to be on the pill was not only extremely unusual but carried a connotation of looseness and immorality.

The issue which faced the establishment and indeed society in general, was the potentially seismic shift in accepted morals. If both men and women wanted to be more sexually active and the pill made this safe for women, then there would be no further inhibition about freely engaging in non-committal sex with anyone you fancied.

It must be so hard for anyone in this day and age to understand the frigid moral code of the time. Young men boasted about how much sex they had experienced when in reality it may have been little or none. Young women denied or downplayed their past experience to shield themselves from censure.

Beth went on, 'I have to tell you that I have a boyfriend back home. We have been going together for three years.' Again I was confused. Until this point there had been no hint that she was not free to develop an ongoing relationship with me.

'My boyfriend is not posh,' she said. 'He is a farmer's son. They own several large farms and an agricultural construction company, all of which he will one day inherit.' As if rubbing salt into the wound, she went on to say that her boyfriend drove an expensive sports car. An 'E' type Jaguar, which at the time was the "must-have" accessory for pop stars and the wealthy.

I would like to have pursued this relationship with Beth but learning that there was a long-term boyfriend with good prospects created an awkward situation.

On returning to England, I had to visit the factory

and stayed briefly with my old landlady. While there I purchased a 45 rpm record of Maria Elena and sent it to Beth with an affectionate letter.

After a week working away in Staffordshire, I returned to G's house and was thrown into turmoil by what she said. 'Some friends of yours came here to see you on Wednesday.' That alone was enough to shock and horrify me as I was so ashamed of where I lived I never gave anyone the address.

'Who were they?' I stammered. 'A man and woman' said G. She could not remember the man's name but the girl was called Beth.

Reprehensibly, my next question was, 'Did you tell them who you were?' Greatly relieved that she had not revealed any type of relationship, I enquired as to what they wanted and what they had said.

'Oh they weren't here very long,' indicated G. 'Said they were friends and had just popped in to see you. They did have a nice car. It was bright red.'

I had understood when Beth told me she had a boyfriend she was also giving me a firm message. This was a summer fling - not the real thing. And by the code of the day I realised she would not expect me to interfere in a long-term relationship with good marriage prospects.

Given that Beth lived in Norfolk and had travelled at least 150 miles I knew that they had not merely "popped-in". Why on earth had Beth told her boyfriend about me? Had he questioned her on her return from holiday? Or had she felt the need for some kind of confession?

Had the boyfriend seen the photograph which was included with the record or had he seen the record itself and wondered about it? When I sent these they were intended only as a reminder of what had genuinely been an enjoyable and fun-filled week.

Or, was this on my part a subconscious attempt to hold on to her? Oh God I thought, what a mess, and it's all my fault. Hardest of all to understand was why Beth and her boyfriend had appeared unexpectedly at my lodgings?

I would love to have seen Beth under any different circumstances but was greatly relieved not to have been in the vicinity when they came. Confrontation always scared me and the idea of greeting Beth in that deplorable house in the company of an older, confident, long-term, shot-gun-toting boyfriend completely unnerved me.

My clammy hands shook; I could not concentrate on anything and became very depressed. That evening I could think of nothing else. I tossed and turned through the night trying to understand the situation and what I should do. Finally interpreting this visit as a showdown by the boyfriend who either wanted to get Beth to choose between us or more likely to tell me in front of Beth to piss off.

I felt so dejected; a double loser who had lost Beth and been out-manoeuvred by her confident boyfriend. Unsure how to respond, especially in a way that would protect my fragile ego, I cravenly did nothing and made no further contact with Beth.

The winter of 1962 – 1963 was the coldest since 1895. Almost unheard of, the sea froze offshore beyond the kilometre-long pier at Herne Bay. I was working in London during the first week of December and encountered what was probably the last of the notorious London "smogs".

Fog was a regular occurrence in London but was particularly severe at this time. What made London different was the fog trapped the smoke which poured out of half a million coal fires. Despite wrapping scarves over their faces everyone who ventured out choked and coughed on the foul-smelling, sulphurous smog. Visibility was so reduced there were times when you could barely see more than a few yards.

I distinctly remember carefully crossing the Strand and entering the Charing Cross hotel. In the men's washroom I could see black soot covered my face and filled my nostrils.

Fortunately the approach of my second Christmas at the factory gave me something else to think about. Each year, the company brought in its salesman from around the country for the annual sales meeting. This filled a blank period during which the businesses to whom they sold were all too busy to place orders.

In total, there were about twenty salesmen and the sales-management staff. I was the youngest person not only to have a sales territory but also to have worked in several of them, albeit for short periods of time.

After the final afternoon of meetings there was an open bar, which for most of the men, was the highlight of the gathering. With so many salesmen descending on the factory they had to back in and park at a 45-degree angle, down one side of the long, narrow dispatch road.

Part of the dispatch area included a high, covered portico under which trucks would drive to be gravity loaded from a hopper. Hanging down on either side from this, suspended by long steel cables were two heavy counterweights which operated the hopper-door mechanism.

There was a long-standing company myth that these weights could be pulled out to either side and allowed to swing inwards until they almost touched in the middle. Although never attempted by any of them, the salesman all claimed they could time a drive-through of the swinging weights without the car being hit.

I who had not had anything to drink but was hyped-up by the proceedings and wanted to prove myself, decided in an uncharacteristic fit of bravado, to do it.

It all happened so quickly and without any real planning. All the salesmen, well fortified with free gin, were loudly shouting encouragement. Two of them then set the weights swinging. Heart racing, now in position, concentrating intently I watched a couple of sequences and then gunned the car through the portico.

I almost made it...

But there was a sickening thud at the right rear end of the Hillman. My heart sank as I realized the gravity of what I had done. The other salesmen, all of whom had until that moment been providing raucous and complicit encouragement instantly became mute and raced Le Mans style to their cars. They departed the scene of our shared stupidity in such haste that they very nearly caused a pile-up at the dispatch-yard gate.

The thin-lipped, permanently severe looking, no-nonsense sales-manager glowered at me before dishing out a mega bollocking. He yelled sarcastically, 'It was a company car with which you were entrusted, not a bloody fairground dodgem.'

I was sent to a meeting with the anguished and kindly, but now painfully disillusioned personnel manager. Somewhat housemaster-like he tut-tutted and rambled on a bit about letting people down.

Most painful of all was when I encountered the chairman in one of the production halls. Wearing his trademark, military-cut pinstripe suit, the normally affable and avuncular Sir John gave me a disdainful look, and without speaking turned on his heel and walked away.

Amazingly and inexplicably I was not actually fired. However, the potentially golden boy was now severely tarnished. The Pyrrhic glamour of field assignments came to an abrupt halt as I was sentenced to incarceration in corporate purgatory, otherwise known as the credit department.

Here I worked directly with the credit manager whose philosophy was that the glass is always half empty. This gaunt man's only topic of conversation other than credit-worthiness was about his ongoing battle with greenfly in his mother's garden. But never once did he praise their scent or the beauty of the roses he sought to protect.

He was so ultra-cautious it was surprising any business had an account with our company. My guess was that if the Bank of England wished to open an account it would take him three weeks to agonise over his decision. Even then he would rubber-stamp the file "Probationary Account – Limited Credit Only."

Bad enough my foolishness had deposited me in this depressing environment but I also had to endure the ignominy, the smirking laughter, the sniggering of the office girls as I went into the staff canteen. Yet there was a positive side as well. My Freudian stupidity gave me the opportunity to think about what I really wanted to do.

There was always the option of taking the Australian government's "Populate or Perish" £10 passage offer. The problem with that was the requirement to stay in Australia for a minimum of two years or the traveller would be required to pay the full cost of the outward trip as well as their return: it felt like a potential trap.

Another option was to go to the United States

which seemed to be so rich and prosperous. Based on the latter rather simplistic thinking, I visited the US Embassy on Grosvenor Square and applied for a visa which would allow me to work in the USA for up to two years. But getting such a visa was an unpredictable lottery.

Some weekends I would go to London and stay with my school friend Tony. His grotty little bedsit was so threadbare and Spartan it could have been used as a stage set for a 1960s production of "La Boheme".

He shared this accommodation with another medical student called Sanjeev. The latter said he really wanted to become an actor but when he told his father he was advised in no uncertain terms that the word was pronounced "doctor".

Tony told me about a medical lecture in which the tutor, hoping to secure the students' attention, started with a little humour. 'It always amazes me,' the doctor said, 'that it seems to take hours for a woman to get dressed and yet in the consulting room they can strip off pretty quickly.

'One woman asked me where she should put her clothes. I said just put them down in the corner - on top of mine.'

On another occasion the psychiatrist giving a lecture, noticed that one of the female students was knitting. Arrogantly, he looked directly at her and said, 'Knitting is merely a sublimation for masturbation.'

Without a pause she shot back, 'When I knit I knit, and when I masturbate I masturbate.'

I did go to a few parties in the London flat of some girls I had met. All the girls were so lovely and spoke with highly acceptable accents, which in their case originated from Rhodesia. They exuded confidence in part created by generous allowances from their affluent parents all of whom seemed to own farms the size of Dorset.

Most of the girls in this set had been to school in England, many of them having attended Roedean which at that time was considered to be the premier girls' school. Physically, Roedean is housed in an austere structure overlooking the sea in East Sussex. The girls all referred to it as Colditz-on-the Cliffs.

During the war, British servicemen were billeted in this school. It was a source of amusement to them, that in many of the rooms there was a bell over which a sign read, 'Press if you require a mistress.'

The walls of the girls' apartment, like those of many other young women in London, were decorated with posters of Rudolf Nureyev and Che Guevara, icons of the time. I could and should have enjoyed these gatherings but instead felt unable to keep up with the affluence and the expectations I assumed these girls would have about potential boyfriends.

I had managed to save nearly £200, a not insubstantial sum of money for that time. For better or worse, post-war austerity and a strict upbringing had taught me the rare, and in my case perhaps dubious skill, of deferring gratification. Moreover, I was able to resume my passion for traditional jazz, played live in nearby Windsor.

During one such Friday night session, when Terry Lightfoot was performing, I met a group of young office workers from the company. They had already had a few beers and were in jolly mood.

They offered a warm welcome celebrating me as the hero who had courageously attempted to slay the mythical beast of the swinging weights. They did not think of me as an idiot who had damaged a company car and thrown away his career under such ridiculous circumstances.

One of the girls was slim, pretty and vivacious. We had chatted and smiled a bit in the office but as Christine already had a long-term boyfriend there was no more to it than that. It did not, however, stop me from looking out for her. As she scampered around the large, un-partitioned general office we would try to make eye-contact and she would always smile.

A few weeks later I told her about receiving a visa and my proposed departure to the United States. Her smile evaporated: I thought she was going to burst into tears. Instead, she turned quickly and rushed away. Could it be that...

I now had £190, every penny of which I had earned and saved. This was to take me to the US and if possible to other places as well. The Far East perhaps? There were two options for getting to New York. The cheapest airfare was approximately one hundred pounds on Icelandic Airways via Reykjavik and Labrador.

The second was to travel by ship which would cost about the same and provide a few days travel on an ocean liner. Having seen the imposing Art Deco 1930s poster of the Normandie and movies depicting the quasi country-house interiors of liners, I thought it would be very grand. I even wondered if I should take my dinner jacket for all those formal occasions.

Sometimes it is only much later in life we recognise what people have seen in us and what they have done for us. So it was with Mrs. Nicholson, the Irish extrovert, chain-smoking doctor's wife and occasional visitor to the rectory.

Her confidence was such she did not pay overdue attention to her appearance. Her straight, greying hair received minimal attention and she could look quite forbidding in her heavy tweed suit. Every time she saw me she bellowed out the same enthusiastic greeting:

'How is my handsome torchbearer today?' I did not understand this flamboyant salutation but because of the jovial way in which it was shouted, and because it contained the word handsome, I took it as a compliment.

When I was about thirteen, Mrs. Nicholson had dispatched me with her similarly-aged daughter, to a fun-fair which was visiting the town. She gave me a pound and hoped we would both enjoy ourselves. At the end of the evening, much to the annoyance of Mrs. Nicholson's daughter, we had only been on one ride and I returned the majority of the money to Mrs Nicholson. She was surprised by this gesture, knowing that any money she had ever given to her children never yielded change.

But through this action she understood the repressive training I had received. She knew that the natural joy, guiltless pleasure and happiness her own children exuded, had been excised from me and replaced with a dour sense of obligation and duty.

On the day before my departure, March 5th 1964, Mrs. Nicholson came to the rectory to see her handsome torchbearer. She gave me an envelope which was to be opened later and wished me bon voyage. She also said, 'I shall never see you again. When you have tasted freedom in the United States you will not wish to return to England and the restrictions you have been under.

The envelope contained two important things, the first and most obvious being the crisp five pound note.

Five pounds was a generous gesture on her part and a welcome addition to the £90 with which I was setting off.

Of greater value in the long-term, was the hand written note she had enclosed. It read,

'I have no doubt you will have a wonderful time. You will have so many new experiences and meet many interesting people. May life be good to you.' Beneath she had copied out a quotation from Hamlet, the significance of which, we both understood was pertinent to me.

"This above all: To Thine Own Self be True, and it must follow, as the night the day, thou canst not then be false to any man. Farewell."

BOOK 2

Chapter 3

THE SEA VOYAGE

'Are you going far?' asked the woman sitting opposite me on the train. 'About three thousand miles,' I said proudly. 'I'm going to New York.'

What it would be like I really had no idea; that was exactly why I wanted to travel. To peer round corners, to pass through hidden gates, to feel the tingling excitement of secret, moon-lit passage-ways. Although perhaps it was a little unrealistic to think I would experience these in New York.

Grappling my way onto a double-decker bus in Liverpool I did not look like the Adventurer and Explorer I felt myself to be. Struggling with my well-worn, poor-quality, expandable suitcase and the small tartan plastic holdall in which I had carried cheese sandwiches and two apples.

Under one arm I carefully protected the large, elaborately wax-sealed manila envelope containing my chest X-ray and US visa. The American embassy staff had warned that if the X-ray or seal were in any way damaged they would be unacceptable and I would not be admitted into the USA.

Overall these accoutrements did not contribute to the image I would like to have portrayed. Henry Morton Stanley crossing the African continent with his long line of bearers in search of Dr. Livingstone, had been much more successful in creating an imposing image.

The bus deposited me some way from the correct pier but that did not matter as it was to be a couple of hours before anyone was allowed to board the ship. Cold and tired, I sat on the suitcase in the murky, cheerless embarkation hall waiting for time to pass. As I waited, I wondered if this really was such a good idea. After all, I might not like it in America, I might dislike the people and if I did not find work would quickly run out of money.

Commendably I did not dwell on these possibilities, cheering myself up with the fact that money was not really a problem. After all, even after paying for the ship's passage, visa costs and rail fares I still had £90, including the five pounds which Mrs. Nicholson had given me. In England I could live for ages on that amount. Even if the US was twice as expensive, I reckoned I could survive for about nine weeks.

Slowly, the endless formalities were completed and I started to walk up the gangplank of the Cunard liner, *Sylvania*. I thought to myself that this must surely be one of those life-changing moments that would forever remain in my memory.

As if playing the film-part of a soldier going off to war, I briefly paused to take a melodramatic look over my shoulder at my homeland: the country I was leaving and to which I might never return. Well, actually what I looked at was the dusty old embarkation hall.

The ship was a vast rabbit warren, suitcases lining every corridor and staircase: people anxiously searching for their luggage with an urgency normally exhibited only in the pursuit of lost children.

Built in 1957, this was the last Cunard vessel specifically designed for the purpose of transporting people back and forth across the North Atlantic. It was in two classes, first and tourist, with the latter accounting for at least 90% of the passengers.

I was greatly impressed with my cabin. All the varnished wood, small shower-room-WC and four beds with little ladders to the upper bunks, all arranged so compactly. Most of all I liked the polished brass fitting around the porthole. Pretty luxurious I thought, for tourist class.

As tugboats pulled the huge ship onto the evening tide, a wall of passengers three of four deep pressed against the starboard gunwale. They waved excitedly to their loudly-cheering friends and relatives on the quayside. The awareness that I had no one to wave to and that there was no one waving to me brought a ripple of melancholy. Oh that recurring, hollowed-out feeling of loneliness.

My parents could have driven me to Liverpool but that was not the way they did things. Their attitude was that if I was going all the way to America, getting myself to Liverpool was just a part of that journey. So in customary fashion, I had simply shaken hands with my father when he dropped me off at Exeter St Davids.

My two cabin-mates were amiable chaps. One was a telephone installer going to Canada to look for work, after which he would send for his family. The other caused some confusion because he said he was a student from Alberta.

He must be very rich I thought, because of his high-quality leather luggage and beautiful toilet set. Also I did not know of any university students who could afford to take a year's break just to travel.

On the first night there was a dance in the main lounge. The band played one number after another but nobody danced. We all sat around in little groups with our cabin-mates, nervously watching everyone else.

Disappointed I felt none of the girls looked like good material for a shipboard romance.

Rather annoyingly, I then learned that the ship was not sailing straight out to sea but was going to Glasgow first to pick up more passengers. After this it was going to Halifax, Nova Scotia prior to docking in New York. Details which the travel agent who sold me the ticket failed to mention.

The following day everyone was assigned to a table for lunch and dinner. I determined to make a good impression on the people with whom I would spend so many, hopefully enjoyable hours. Despite the fact that we were still within sight of land and the sea was as calm as a millpond, there was one empty seat at the table. We were informed the lady who should have occupied it, - was seasick.

My other table companions consisted of a pleasant Yorkshire couple in their 50s and a half-witted young man who had been their lodger. The thought of looking for new lodgings apparently terrified him so much that, selecting the lesser of two evils, he decided to emigrate to the US with them. There was also a woman in her mid-30s who smiled nervously but said nothing.

They were all nice people, but where was I to find the provocative conversation that would make me laugh and stimulate me? To my right sat a not unattractive woman of about 26.

'Where are you from?' I asked cheerily.

'Wheels,' she said

'Where's that?' I asked

'Don't you know where Wales is man?' she snapped

'Oh, Wales!' I said, disappointed in my final dining companion and turning scarlet from my stupidity and her fiery retort.

After lunch, selecting a book at random from the library, I sat in the main lounge hoping that if anything was to going to happen, it would happen there. Following a couple of hours of complete boredom I even started to read the book.

Then, remembering the substantial notebook I had brought with me to be used as a diary I wondered if I would experience anything sufficiently worthwhile to write in it. What I did not want was to end my life like Anton Chekhov's eponymous "Uncle Vanya". A husk of a man looking back at a mundane, unfulfilled life.

'So this is where you are hiding,' came a voice from behind. I turned just as the Welsh woman dropped into the seat beside me. She was smiling and attractive; more feminine than the glowering schoolmarm at the dining table.

'What's your name?' I asked. 'Anwen' she replied.

I did not hear the name properly but had no intention of asking her to repeat it. We spent the afternoon together and even went to the post-dinner dance together. Next morning I set out to look for her. The following nights found me going to bed progressively later. Those evenings were spent drinking the tax-free beer and dancing.

As the ship's public areas started to close down late at night, the two of us would walk round the deck waiting for everybody else to go to bed. We would then sit in a corner of the lounge or the library, huddling together as the heat dwindled.

We chatted but also became comfortable being together in silence. Gradually, as the cleaners and stewards arrived to do their work, we were shuffled from one stateroom to another. Although the clocks were put back an hour each night it was usually 3.30

or 4 a.m. before I climbed into bed. Even then I was still thinking about Wen.

Her cabin, which of course she shared with other women, was off a minor companionway which afforded some privacy when we said good night. Each night the kissing lasted a little longer and became more torrid.

As we pressed together against the wall I would have given anything for a cabin of my own. It was Wen who reminded me that my cabin mates were disembarking at Halifax. She declared, that for the two nights en route to New York, she would be tucking me into bed.

Not fitted with stabilisers, the ship seemed to roll all the time. This became most apparent when people were on the dance floor. They migrated en-masse from one side of the room to the other, much to the amusement of the seated non-dancers.

One day there was a really bad storm which must have caught the crew by surprise because it sent plates flying off the tables at lunchtime. Within an hour ropes had been put up along all the passageways, so those brave enough to venture out could hang on.

A couple of nervous passengers - presumably remembering the Titanic - loudly informed everyone within earshot that the ship was of course in the dangerous North Atlantic, an area abundant with icebergs.

I talked to as many people as possible, especially the returning Americans. On many occasions I asked people how much money I could earn. $60 (£24 a week) sounded like a generous figure, but after all, this was America land of the rich and birthplace of the American dream. A dream in which I visualised myself driving one of those huge, outrageously-finned automotive monsters.

Like most young people I did not think seriously about the future; well not the long-term future anyway. But I did hope that in some way I could rise above the general anticipation that the trajectory of my life appeared to be heading only towards mediocrity.

On the day prior to arrival in Halifax there were some pre-landing checks requiring everyone to produce their passport. Wen looked aghast when she glimpsed mine. 'Surely you are not only twenty?' she said incredulously. 'No you cannot see my passport; it is private,' she went on. This started a quarrel leading to her saying she was embarrassed by the age difference, before eventually admitting that she was twenty-eight.

This did not worry me as I was secretly rather proud of the fact that at my age I was able to attract someone older and so much more worldly.

Arrival time in Halifax approached. Excitement throughout the ship was palpable. About 6 A.M. I had slipped quietly out of my bunk and looked through the porthole. All I could see was a row of dim lights along a cold, fog-enshrouded wharf. Nothing beautiful, nothing different to anything I had seen before, but I felt a surge of unrestrained excitement.

This was the vast country of Canada coloured "Empire pink" on all the out-dated, wall-hung maps at which I had stared at my prep school. Stories of General Wolfe and his heroic victory at the Plains of Abraham heralded all the new adventures for which I yearned.

For those disembarking to start a new life in Canada, it was the end of a carefree interregnum. The real challenges of settling in a new country were now becoming a reality. The normally placid telephone repair man admitted to me that he felt so sick and nervous he would not be able to eat any breakfast.

The quiet routine of the ship changed to one of frenetic activity. Everyone became animated, with numerous passengers rushing to undertake suddenly important business. Others formed orderly but excited queues at the Purser's office, chirping to each other like birds on a telephone wire.

Many people still had long journeys ahead of them. The university student said, 'It will take me three days non-stop train travel to reach Calgary.' When you come from a small island like Britain, it is hard to imagine a piece of land so large that it takes days of non-stop train travel to cross.

Some of the New York-bound passengers walked into the centre of Halifax. All of us were ill-prepared for the wet slush through which we walked. The young men were disappointed by the cars we saw. Yes they were indeed large, but mostly in poor condition and dirty as a result of the salt and slushy snow. Nothing like the gleaming chrome-encrusted, candy-red Cadillacs I had seen in the glossy National Geographic advertisements.

Throughout dinner that night, and the dancing that followed, I was anticipating what would happen later. Due to my naiveté I did not leave the dance before it ended but did eliminate the ritual stroll around the deck.

I understood Wen's clear intention, but was for some reason nervous. This was somehow different to the format I had experienced with girls of my own age and I was unsure of the etiquette involved under these circumstances.

After some heavy embracing, Wen gently said,

'I promised to tuck you into bed so shall now do so.' Stripping down to my underpants I slipped into the bunk. More confidently Wen removed her dress and joined me.

Wishing to impress her as a great lover I certainly did not intend to fail for lack of foreplay. At last Wen could stand it no longer and cried out, 'What are you waiting for man? Put it in!'

Somewhat taken aback, I did so.

She praised me, saying how good I was. That was exactly the reassurance I needed and had the result of rebuilding my ardour time after time. At yet another fresh approach, Wen remarked incredulously, 'What, again? You really are a quick re-loader!'

I took this as a sign of success and fell asleep glowing with pride, but thinking it would have been nice to have had one more shot.

Breakfast over, I sauntered around the ship looking for someone to talk to. As I leaned over the stern guardrail I thought of the previous night. I had really been good: my initiation with an older woman completed, I was now truly a man.

Only seven days ago I was in the old life. Now everything had changed. I had cut former ties and things were moving on. I had already had a transatlantic sea voyage, visited Canada and was in the process of having an intense affair. Life could not have been better.

After the dance on the final night of the voyage there were numerous parties held in different parts of the ship. Wen and I circulated around these before a large group packed into my tiny cabin. Everyone was laughing and good-humoured.

Although there were no other couples, the close proximity created a wonderful intimacy. When everyone finally departed well after 4 A.M. having exchanged contact details which were unlikely ever to be used, there were only a couple of hours before we needed to `prepare for disembarkation.

Despite having drunk a fair amount, nothing could dampen my enthusiasm or my ability to perform. Wen was gentle and carefree with me, enjoying my youthful energy. In an ideal world she would probably have preferred a little less quantity and a little more quality to the lovemaking.

Chapter 4

ARRIVAL in NEW YORK

Walking down the gang plank in New York was an anti-climax. The large hangar-like reception building we entered looked exactly the same as the one from which we had departed in Liverpool.

The difference was that having emerged from the un-demanding chrysalis of the ship the passengers were now animated and excited.

This was the start of a new day and a new chapter in their lives. As we jostled noisily among ourselves we quite literally created a little dust storm, the particles visible in light columns beneath the ceiling-hung, high-intensity industrial lights.

I made my way down the alphabet line of tables to a large K, the first letter of my surname, where I was required to fill in numerous forms, all of which seemed irrelevant. One question asked, 'Are you entering the country for illegal or immoral purposes?' I thought that was particularly ridiculous, doubting the Kray twins or Christine Keeler would tick yes to that one.

There was also a requirement to fill in a registration form for the American Draft. A scary reminder that the United States was starting to send a new generation of young men to a distant country most of them had never heard of, to fight in a war they neither understood, nor wanted. The very idea that the Americans would draft me, a British citizen, into the Army seemed preposterous and remote.

So many foolish questions answered, so many forms already completed, this seemed like just another formality.

Waiting for my baggage I noticed groups of young people much my own age, greeting the new arrivals. Some of the girls looked quite nice but none of them came up and asked who I was or where I was going. Perhaps it was because the letter 'K' put me so noticeably in the centre of the arrivals hall. Perhaps it was that as a young man on my own I was too obvious a target.

Then one girl, clipboard in hand, bravely marched up and introduced herself as Janie. 'I am part of the volunteer team greeting new arrivals and offering assistance. As a new immigrant is there anything I can do to help you?' she enquired.

Surprised and somewhat confused, I failed to respond coherently but Janie was obviously well-prepared as she pressed a piece of paper into my hand saying, 'You must take my 'phone number just in case there is something you need.'

I did not think of myself as an immigrant; nor was I part of the unwashed 'huddled masses' arriving at Ellis Island. Yes, I did have an 'Immigrant' visa but that was to fulfil the requirement which would allow me to work.

Wen was travelling to Boston, to take up a nursing position. Understood but ill-defined was the notion that we would be continuing our relationship. For better or worse, we were together in a country where neither of us knew anyone, not conscious of it, but both having need of the other.

As we stood on the platform beside the train, Wen

pressed into me and with watery eyes looked up and said, 'You're a funny bloke. Half man, half boy. I hope New York knocks the corners off you without killing you in the process.'

'You calling me funny?' I said. 'That's a bit rich coming from a wacky Welsh woman like you.' We laughed out of nervous tension as Wen's train pulled away: both emotionally depleted and physically exhausted.

This being before the invention of wheeled suitcases I had to carry my heavy bag as I walked through the aptly named Grand Central station. Its vast hall and impressively high ceiling echoing like a cathedral. Peering at its splendour I was almost knocked over by a young clergyman, who at great speed leapt down the broad staircase four steps at a time.

His obviously fictitious clerical attire fell off revealing an orange sweatshirt depicting cartoon characters. He paused long enough to pick up his phoney ecclesiastical garb and shove it back on before disappearing with equal haste into the crowd. What kind of a madhouse is this place I thought!

Inside the subway I politely asked someone which train line I should take for 34th Street. Without replying the man just stood there looking through me as if I did not exist. I then asked someone else, who sidestepped and walked away eyeing me suspiciously.

The station walls were heavy with soot and some people uninhibitedly threw cardboard cups and chewing gum onto the tracks as if that is what they were there for. The heat was oppressive and the ancient trains rattled so violently it seemed they would disintegrate into a pile of scrap metal.

Far in the distance, many blocks down the long straight thoroughfare, I could see giant letters vertically spelling out YMCA, my intended home for the foreseeable future. Sloane House was well located at 356 West 34th Street, the largest residential YMCA building in the US and, therefore, presumably in the world.

The iconic Empire State building was also visible but I was disappointed by its size. In my imagination, it was stratospherically tall soaring high into the ionosphere.

About to walk over a crossroads I saw a motorist who had stopped to work out the slightly confusing traffic system. The impatient taxi behind her, protected by his extra "bull-bar" fenders, just pushed her forwards at what appeared to be an alarming speed.

Further on I saw two women parking a Cadillac in a space only marginally longer than the car itself. They damaged the Corvair in front, bending the fender and leaving one tail-light pointing at an odd angle.

Why was it that I had encountered and witnessed so many acts of rudeness and selfishness? This confused and disoriented me: it was all so different to sleepy Seavale.

Entering the landmark fourteen-story YMCA I joined a long queue for one of the many reception desks. People of all ages and ethnicities milled around but the feeling I had was that the majority of people there were neither young nor Christian.

At the reception desk I was greeted by the single word, 'Yeah?' It was cordial enough and presumably was both a greeting and a question as to what I wanted. The cheapest accommodation was $2.50 for a room per night. Outrageous! That was nearly one pound a night or seven pounds a week. Equivalent to the take home pay of many families in England.

The only way to reach the rooms was by taking one

of the six elevators, all of which seemed to be operated by cretins. Entering the elevator I had to produce my room key and even then I was scrutinised suspiciously by one of the distinctly odd looking, slow-paced operators.

As they moved the selection lever through its 180° arc, they all appeared to relish their authority as controller of a lift. Probably the only recognition accorded to them in their otherwise invisible lives.

On the sixth floor I walked down a dim corridor lit only by artificial light, past rows of identical, closely-spaced doors. Finding my room I edged past the bed and laid down my bags.

The cell-like room contained only the bare essentials, but did look clean and there was a telephone hanging high on the wall. In the many hotels in which I had stayed, none had the luxury of a telephone in the guest room, only a public pay-phone by the reception desk.

The window was in proportion to the room and consequently offered very little light. Able only to poke my head through, I peered out and could see the building was a quadrangle and that my window faced the narrow inner courtyard.

Looking up I could not see the sky: looking down I saw a mesh screen at the bottom of the well, littered with empty cans and garbage. Before withdrawing, my head was narrowly missed by a descending food can, its jagged lid catching the air causing it to spin.

Walking to the washroom I was sickened to see the drinking-fountain bowl full of spittle and sputum. In the washroom I noticed a man loitering but it was only when I turned round from the urinal I realised that this seedy character had been watching me in the mirror.

Disgusted, disillusioned and completely exhausted, I returned to my room and collapsed onto the bed. So

this was America, the supposedly fabulous country of
my dreams. Dirty, noisy and populated by undesirables
and low-life! What foolishness had brought me here?

Chapter 5

EARLY DAYS IN NY

My slumber was shattered by a piercingly loud sound. Finally realising it was the phone I struggled up and groggily reached for the receiver. It was Brenda, a beautiful suntanned blonde girl who worked in the Bahamas and had been in my loose circle of the acquaintances on the ship.

'Several of us are going up the Empire State building tonight,' she said. 'You will come won't you?' I could not have been happier. Somebody wanted to make contact with me - I had a friend in New York.

In the foyer of the Empire State building I recognised a nurse called Jane and several of the other people, including a broad-shouldered giant of a boy whom I had seen but not really spoken to on the ship.

'You know Jim and the others don't you?' said Brenda. Realising then that although I had seen all these people and spoken to some of them many times, I had foolishly not taken the trouble to engage with them. My narrow focus had been on Wen to the exclusion of getting to know so many other interesting young people.

Through the course of the evening I learned that Jim was also lodging at Sloane House. 'Oh, you're staying in that shit-hole as well are you?' was his observation. As Jim was also looking for work we decided to join forces. Together, we determined to take New York by storm. Well-motivated I rose early next morning and bought a paper to look for job vacancies. There were many advertised but it was obvious that we could not rush all over the city investigating these.

Deciding to go to an employment agency we filled in numerous forms, undertook some peculiar pictorial IQ tests and were finally told we were unsuitable for any jobs listed with that agency. The routine and outcome was the same with other agencies and so, much deflated, we returned to the YMCA.

Determined to conserve money we avoided using the subway and walked everywhere. I disliked the communal YMCA lounge with its creepy characters and had walked enough during the day not to want to go out again. That evening after a frugal supper I went straight to bed.

The next couple of days were spent in the same way with the same results. One employment agency would not interview Jim because he was not wearing a tie. I was turned down because the only jobs they had were with finance companies. Walking down Fifth Avenue on day four, the mid-March wind was so bitterly cold that like the dispossessed immigrants we were, we took refuge in the imposing "Great Library" just to warm up. My confidence was ebbing away as I started to think about my diminishing financial resources and wondering what my alternatives might be. 'Let's forget about agencies and office work, said Jim. 'I wouldn't mind being a chauffeur or something like that.'

So while he went for an interview on the East Side, I returned to my room and phoned a couple of people whose names I had been given in England and who might be able to help me find work. My contacts were cordial and supportive but nothing in the way of work seemed forthcoming.

We had heard that the impending New York World's Fair would create many employment opportunities, so we went to Queens to enquire about jobs as security guards or bus drivers. We were told we could not be security guards because we were not American citizens and that Jim, at six foot five, could not be a bus driver because they did not have any uniforms in his size.

It was now almost routine that seeing an employment agency I would walk in, complete the forms, say my piece, be told that they had nothing for me and leave. But this one was different. 'D'ya know anything about chemistry?' said the interviewer in his New Jersey accent.

'Certainly, studied it for years,' I said with absolutely nothing to lose. Expecting then to be asked a few technical questions which of course I would not be able to answer, that would be the end of it.

But it wasn't. I was told to come back the next day for an interview. Still expecting to be stumped by technical questions I returned to the office the following day after normal business hours. About fifteen or twenty young men were waiting to be interviewed. An odd assortment of characters, but one which represented the ethnic diversity of the city.

Into the middle of this group strutted a man whom I could only describe as sartorially pretentious. This Beau Brummel character was wearing an immaculate, near-black, three-piece suit, a white tab-shirt of the style much favoured on Wall Street at the time and displaying a mirror-like shine on his formal black shoes. Worst of all, not a single blond hair of his wavy main was out of place. As if set in concrete his smile revealed pearly white teeth which contrasted with his somewhat orange-tinged suntan.

Mr. Schneider simply effervesced vitality and locking

his eyes onto mine said 'Tell me ALLLL about yourself.'

He was particularly interested in my description of the strict English boys' school I had attended, presumably believing the stereotypical inaccuracies that such institutions were rife with beatings and buggery.

By now I was well aware that completing college was the recognised baseline of education in America in the same way that A-levels were in the United Kingdom. Trying to offset my lack of a degree, I talked-up my management training with the food company. Mr. Schneider quickly came back on track and enquired, 'What do you know about chemistry?'

Gambling that Mr. Schneider was some kind of personnel manager and probably did not know a lot about chemistry himself, I replied, 'I know a little about molecular chemistry but am somewhat rusty on my analytical.'

Grimacing to indicate that he recognised bullshit when he heard it he went on, 'Did you ever undertake any experiments?' 'Oh frequently, I said not wishing to confuse the issue by mentioning how basic my General Science 'O' level had been.

Leaving the employment agency I was still not sure exactly what I had applied for. I only knew that it was something to do with mixing chemicals at the New York World's Fair. It had, however, been an interesting exercise and who knew, it might even lead to something.

Anyway at six foot two, I was not too tall to be fitted with a bus driver's uniform.

Next morning, in compliance with the terms of my American visa, I had to go uptown for my Draft Board medical examination. Had I been deemed medically unfit for military service that would have been an end to the matter. Being declared healthy meant that I and anyone else on the Draft Board register, would simply wait until the lottery called them for mandatory military service.

The examination was held in an ancient building which was physically and aesthetically cold and dark. All the windows had been covered over not only eliminating natural light but, effectively severing our ties with the normality of the world outside.

The uniformed army personnel were deliberately intimidating, shouting loudly at everyone and ordering us around as if we were already in the Army. The hard-faced men conducting these medical tests, obviously did so day-in and day-out. They were as routine and callous as ranchers dealing with cattle.

All potential draftees were required to strip naked. A medical orderly walked down the line sticking his fingers into our pubic area, telling us to look away and cough. He did not change his gloves between these examinations and so if the first man in the line had either crabs or herpes it would theoretically be possible for the orderly to "single-handedly" infect the whole group.

We were instructed to turn around, legs apart, bend over and touch our feet. Another orderly came along the line, and sparing no indignity, pulled my buttocks apart to more closely examine my anus. Was this horrible ordeal really necessary or did they deliberately set out to destroy the last vestige of our dignity and self-respect?

A medic went down the line, sort of wiping his stethoscope across our chests. I cannot believe the stethoscope was held long enough for him to have heard anything relevant. Finally, we were given what looked like strips of litmus paper and sent into the lavatory to pee on them. The man next to me simply dipped his litmus paper into the trough.

When at last we were released back into the daylight and civilian life this man was walking towards the subway station. 'Why did you dip your litmus paper into the trough rather than pee on it?' I enquired.

'Can't pee in front of other people. Don't know why but if anybody else is around it just doesn't happen. The medical name for this is paruresis. It is a type of social phobia apparently ranking second only to the fear of public speaking.'

How awful I thought. It would have been impossible to go through all my school years with such a condition. Not only the inconvenience but the constant ridicule.

It came as a relief that night when the group of friends from the ship went to Chinatown. We all found the area delightfully unusual with its pagoda- topped phone booths and large porcelain dragons.

Being with this group and being part of a group, was absolutely the best thing for me and for the others. We had camaraderie and support without which all of us would have been mere orphans in this forbidding, inhospitable city.

Wen and I had already exchanged emotional letters and managed an expensive, ten-minute phone conversation. 'People are all very business-like here,' she said. 'They are welcoming but also busy with work and their own lives. I have not really settled in and feel lonely: I miss you a lot.'

'My job search is not going well,' I reported. 'But I shall keep trying until something comes up. I'm so lucky that Jim is here and how wonderful to have the little group of friends from the ship. I miss you terribly and want so much to be with you again.'

Although Jim had been job-hunting he did not seem overly upset by his lack of progress. He must have had a lot more money than me, because having rightly been informed that used cars were comparatively inexpensive, it was now his intention to buy a car and travel to the west coast.

Then came that magical phone call. The man with the "Joisey" accent informed me that I had been one of six people selected out of eighteen to be given the job. The chemical company, of which I had never heard, would provide appropriate training which was due to start the following Monday.

Almost as an afterthought, Jersey-man mentioned that the salary was $100 per week. I was overjoyed and could hardly believe that I had landed a job paying $100 a week. £40 per week. Over £2000 per year. Far more money than my father had ever earned. I was elated that I had a job and only wished that Jim had been selected as well. But Jim was sanguine as usual. He had his own dreams to fulfil: a road trip via the iconic Route 66 to California, land of the preppy Beach Boys and Surfin' USA.

With the security of a six/seven-month job lined up, I made immediate plans to visit Boston. As Jim had already purchased a car we decided to drive together. Jim let me drive the large Chevrolet with its power steering but never having driven an automatic before there were a couple of times when my left foot embarrassingly hit the wide power-brake pedal.

On arrival in the suburban town near Boston I was thrilled to be with Wen. But there were some logistical problems. Wen shared a one-bedroom flat with another nurse. Under normal circumstances that was not an issue for them because they worked different shifts and did not overlap that much. But two guests in that small flat did create unwanted tension.

Returning to the NY employment agency I was due to collect a railway ticket and expenses for my three days of training. Here I met the five colleagues whom I would get to know well over the coming months. We were all excited because we had all landed a high-paying job at the much-hyped New York World's Fair.

Amazing to me was the apparent confidence and ease with which this disparate group merged together. They joked endlessly and good-naturedly, immediately starting to mimic my English accent. I in turn deliberately overstressed some words which I knew would amuse them.

When telling a joke which involved the word castration I pronounced it car-stration, which they predictably picked up and repeated in exaggerated pseudo-English accents.

I did not mimic their accents because after all I was in their country, but I did learn a whole new vocabulary. Rick cynically disapproved of great swathes of society constantly referring to these people as scumbags.

Bernie and Aaron, who were both Jewish, sounded at times as if they were speaking in a different language. They would kibbitz with each other and would 'schlep on over' rather than go somewhere. People for whom they did not care were either schmucks or schlemiels.

Ridiculous as it sounds, I didn't actually know what a Jew was. Of course I had heard references to Jews in the Bible and knew about the Holocaust but that still did not explain who these people were. The fact that there was an ethnic group who had spread throughout the world with their own religion was not understood by me.

My narrow upbringing confined me to a sense that the Church of England was superior to everything else. Even Catholics and dissenters such as Methodists were treated with some suspicion by my parents. One girl with whom I had a platonic relationship was very dark skinned. When someone said of her, 'I don't know what religion she is, I had no idea what he was implying.

New York was of course the great melting pot, refuge and home to generations of immigrants. All ethnic groups had uncomplimentary names and derogatory terms for the others, although at times these were simply used as descriptors: Kikes, Spicks, Wops, Spades and Honkies. I also heard myself described disparagingly as a Goy and more politely as a Wasp.

The chemical company headquarters totally amazed me; it was a vast establishment with numerous state-of-the-art modern buildings. It could not have been a greater contrast to the antiquated, L.S.Lowry-like brick-built, Victorian food factory with its traditional landmark tall chimney.

Our training was conducted by a friendly if somewhat boring, middle-aged chemistry Ph.D. He in turn was assisted by an amiable but equally bland lab assistant.

The six of us were taught how to mix chemicals and how to prepare the experiments which would be shown on stage in the chemical company's pavilion. It was a relatively simple demonstration designed for visual effect and to promote company products rather than impart any real knowledge of chemistry.

For example, a fresh rose was dipped into Freon, a chlorofluorocarbon which in its liquid state was so cold it caused the rose to instantly freeze solid. At this stage, the demonstrator in gloved hand, would crush the rose in front of the microphone so that the amazed audience could both see and hear the crumbling effect.

Another of the stunts, called the iodine clock, involved mixing two clear, water-like chemicals which could then be timed precisely to turn totally black after a count of ten seconds. Again relatively simple but dramatic. There were also thixotropic materials which could change viscosity from a liquid state to a gel and vice versa which formed the basis of non-drip paints.

Carcinogenic trichloroethylene was used in one of the experiments and from that day on I recognise its distinctive smell every time I enter a dry-cleaning shop.

The luxury of the company hotel in which we stayed was overwhelming. We each had a spacious, well-furnished room complete with television set and a telephone. The pièce de résistance was the large en-suite bathroom with its fluffy towels, selection of toiletries and a second phone.

On the return train journey to New York, I told the group that I would be looking for a place to stay and asked if any of them would like to share with me. It turned out that none of them needed lodgings but the discussion did move on to where I could find an apartment and how much I would have to pay in rent.

None of my group ever referred again to my open offer to share accommodation with my five work colleagues, but there was some significance to it. One of the six trainee chemical prep-boys was an African-American of about twenty, called Jaydon.

This, a mere four years after the Sharpeville massacre and only a few months after Martin Luther King's "I Have a Dream" speech. A time, when even in New York City, there was a two-tier social structure and a strong undercurrent of segregation.

Subsequently, I rented a small, one-bedroom apartment on East 53rd Street with a friendly if somewhat introverted young man called Freddie, whom I had met at the "Y". Freddie, a small-town boy from rural Pennsylvania was impressed with my relative sophistication and polish. Being new to the city and rejecting the human flotsam found in the YMCA, Freddie had not made friends during his two months in New York. He was, therefore, pleased to live vicariously on the edge of my burgeoning social circle.

Because he was taking responsibility for the lease, he had the bedroom and I slept in a sort of alcove which had no door and was open to the corridor. We also hoped we might be able to offset the rent by allowing someone to sleep on the sofa in the living room.

Freddie worked for a large international press agency as a clerk in their photo library. When a picture relating to any news story was required, it was his job to search through the files and select either a specific picture or one with some connection to the story.

Working on a nightshift he invited me to come down and see the offices which were virtually empty at that time. Freddie threw out a challenge saying he could find a picture on any subject I could name. This led to much opening of filing-cabinet drawers and confirmation that amazingly, Freddie could indeed find a picture of almost anything.

After being sworn to total confidentiality he asked if I would like to see the "secret" file. This turned out to contain quite the saddest, most frightening, disgusting and outrageous pictures I had ever seen. There were abhorrent, grotesque and stomach-churning pictures including terrible physical abnormalities, torture victims, battle casualties and the most horribly disfiguring diseases.

There were also a number of pornographic pictures depicting activities of which I had absolutely no knowledge or comprehension. Zoophilia and bestiality featured a few times, including a picture of a woman apparently taking on the dangerous task of masturbating a horse.

Prior to that I had only seen real pornography, as opposed to pin-up pictures, once before. That was at the age of 18 when I met a school-friend in London. He surreptitiously took out an envelope purchased in Soho and showed me half a dozen small black and white photographic prints of an unattractive, middle-aged couple, unimaginatively copulating.

The newly hired group of six had been instructed to go to a "studio" on Sixth Avenue for a briefing. Something to do with the overall show that would take place in the pavilion.

Standing outside was a very tired looking Jaydon. In the process of joining a fraternity, he had undergone hazing, which meant he had been deprived of sleep until 3 A.M. The whole concept of fraternities and the ridiculous initiation process by which they could be joined was completely unknown and anathema to me.

Entering what turned out to be a dance studio was like stepping through a magic door into an exciting world inhabited by beautiful, flamboyant people - A power station generating megawatts of sexuality. The girls were athletic, beautiful and looked incredibly sexy in their leotards and over-the-knee leg-warmers.

All of the dancers, men and women alike, sizzled with raw, uninhibited sensuality. Mr. Schneider was holding forth in the centre of the room. This time dressed casually and as his role now required, theatrically. Deck shoes, tight, mustard-coloured trousers and a peculiar, strangely-cut linen jacket. To complete the effect he had casually draped a powder-blue silk scarf round his neck.

Mr. Schneider, it turned out, did not actually work for the chemical company. He was a theatre director who had secured the contract to stage the production at the chemical company's pavilion.

The pavilion and the production were both multi-faceted, big budget operations employing over 200 people. For a start they engaged about 60 hosts. These were attractive young women and a few men, whose job was to organise the visitors lining up outside the pavilion. They also worked as guides and escorts within the pavilion, carefully channelling the movement of the crowd.

Visitors would line up on both sides of the 180- foot diameter circular pavilion and the two lines would then enter two separate but identical side theatres. Here they would simultaneously see a song and dance routine relating to the end uses of the chemical company's products.

Both these groups then emptied inwards into the large semi-circular Red Room theatre where together 600 people would stand to watch three demonstrators dressed in futuristic 'space-man' white suits going through the chemical stunt routine.

The hostesses were smartly dressed in pale blue blazers and matching skirts topped off with a very '60s style white, space-age hat. In addition to the various costumes of the dancers, there was a band who were always dressed in burgundy blazers and mandatory charcoal trousers. Then there were the six of us whom Mr. Schneider named "the chemical prep-boys". We were all dressed in bright red overall-jumpsuits.

Although obviously impossible, I felt for some strange reason I recognised a couple of the male dancers. Later I was told that they had been Jets in the smash-hit film, West Side Story.

All the male dancers were gay, except one who declared himself to be bisexual. A state Woody Allen thought to be advantageous because it gave a person twice the opportunity to find a date on a Saturday night. Many of the demonstrators, who were all men and had to be theatrical-union card holders, were also gay.

I was thrilled to be in this wonderfully new and exciting environment. Despite my modest backstage role, I sensed the buzz of the production being brought together and was immensely proud to be a part of it. Moreover, being the only English person in this group distinguished me and provided a ready topic of conversation with anyone to whom I spoke.

That evening I went out to dinner with Frank, one of the other prep-boys, an ebullient Italian-American, and his stylish girlfriend. A couple of the other prep- boys were there and the atmosphere was happy and jovial. If there was one thing that concerned me it was that every time I went out with Frank or any of the others, I seemed to spend lots of money. Was it the American way that if you have money you spend it without any thought of saving?

Throughout the following week we and everyone else practised and rehearsed what we were supposed to be doing to get the coordination right. It was not only us; everyone on the fairground was training or rehearsing their role.

Private cars were not allowed onto the fairground but somehow the advertising director of the chemical company always managed to drive right up to the pavilion. He parked his flashy T-Bird convertible ostentatiously in front of the main entrance where everybody would notice it. He was in his mid- 40s, smartly dressed in a corporate sort of a way and permanently smiling, or was it leering at the girls.

One of the reasons there were so many people working at the pavilion was because it operated twelve hours a day, seven days a week. Together, the two side-theatres put on forty-eight shows a day and the central Red Room had twenty-four shows per day, one every half hour.

Before opening it became apparent that some kind of work rota for the prep-boys would have to be established. Surprisingly, it was the hippie Rick, who showed initiative, management skill and common sense in simplifying a timekeeping system.

He was different to the rest of the group in that being 28 was a few years older. Rick described himself as a writer/film-maker with no long-term ambition other than to be creative and support his pregnant, actress wife.

The proposal he put forward was that the six of us should form into three, two-man teams. There would be two shifts per day, which would then require each team to work four days in a row followed by two days off. Much less confusing than the complicated arrangement originally put in place.

Even Mr. Schneider, who had prepared the original and convoluted schedule, could see the wisdom in this. But in his usual theatrical style, had to embellish it by creating three team leaders.

Much to my surprise, I was picked as a team leader, along with Rick and Frank. This promotion carried a salary increase bringing my pay up to a stratospheric

$115 per week. Rightly, however, I was never to collect the full increase. Egalitarian Rick had gone to Mr. Schneider and insisted that all six men should be paid the same amount of $107.50 per week.

If Rick was the most serious and focused of the prep

boys, Frank was unquestionably the social organiser. He suggested I go to a film with him, his girlfriend Yvette and her roommate, Dagmar. I found the elfin Dagmar to be light-hearted and pretty. She had a sweet, gentle nature which allowed her to live comfortably and quietly in Yvette's modelesque shadow without feeling belittled or in any way jealous. I really liked her, but was not romantically interested because of course I had Wen.

With only a week to go before opening, rehearsals became frenetic and nerve-wracking. I was always scared that one of the experiments I had prepared would not work. But there were lighter moments, such as when a mouse ran across the rehearsal room floor.

All the girls screamed but it was the gay men who jokingly jumped the highest and squealed the loudest. So much for the tough-guy gang members from West Side Story!

Contacting the American representative of my former employer, the British food company, led to a dinner invitation for both Jim and I in their lovely mid-Manhattan apartment. He and his wife were so warm and welcoming, showing how kind and generous some Americans could be. They lavished food on us and we laughed, until inevitably one topic was raised:

The assassination of President Kennedy, a mere four months prior to this, was still raw and painful for every American. There was disbelief that anyone, especially an American, would want to kill this wonderful man who was universally loved and admired.

Following the worthy but now seemingly anachronistic style of Dwight and Mamie Eisenhower, the Kennedys had ushered in a new era of youthful confidence and optimism. John F. Kennedy with his film-star good looks and his sophisticated, elegant wife represented the image most Americans wanted their country to portray.

It was difficult to arrange a time when I could visit Wen. We were both working shifts and were both subject to rotas beyond our control. When I did get to Boston a couple of weeks later the conversation did not flow smoothly and things were awkward between us. We did make love rather mechanically, but neither of us seemed to find the excitement we had enjoyed on the ship.

With the benefit of hindsight, my naïveté and to a lesser extent the sense of propriety required by Wen at that time, were probably to blame.

Sex, or "lovemaking" as it was euphemistically called normally took place in a bed at night. There was the common joke about "swinging from the chandelier," but in reality anything other than unimaginative, somewhat serious sex was considered deviant.

At the infamous 1963 divorce trial between the Duke and Duchess of Argyll, part of the evidence included a Polaroid photograph showing fellatio. In reference to this the judge referred to the Duchess as having participated in disgusting sexual activities which he went on to describe as a gross form of sexual relationship and a clear form of perversion.

At the same age as me (twenty) although three years later in 1967, the already married actress Jane Birkin was confiding to her diary about her yearning for experimentation, to have sex standing up, to do it out of doors or in a car: to be desired so urgently and passionately that time and place became irrelevant.

Wen made a comment which worried me: she said

more in earnest than in jest, she was going to 'have me.' My frightened interpretation of this was that, sooner or later, she intended to marry me.

Ten days after that I received a letter from her saying she had been seeing someone in Boston. I was hurt and jealous. Why would she "two-time" the man she had said she would keep for life? Later I realised I should be pleased because I had already told Wen I was not ready to marry anyone.

A week later she came to New York and stayed at the flat. On the night of her arrival we argued about the man she had been seeing in Boston. The following day, we and a few friends went to Central Park to play baseball. It was light-hearted and enjoyable; just the right thing for clearing the air. But that night in bed we argued all over again.

A few days later I phoned her only to experience a very cold reception. A letter which must have been posted prior to the phone call arrived the next day and consisted of a rather catty farewell. Enraged by this letter and Wen's attitude, I immediately tore it up and threw it in the bin.

So ended a six-week affair. Six weeks is such a short space of time and yet it is possible to pack so much emotion into it. So many highs, so many expectations, so many disappointments and a disproportionate amount of turmoil.

Losing Claire had been painful, but now I felt hurt and let down in a different way. This was more about my bruised ego than the loss of a woman with whom I was clearly incompatible. It was confusing that only a short time ago she had been saying she wanted to be my mistress and wife.

At the age of twenty, all life is a mystery, but the intertwining complexities of sex, romance and relationships are the hardest things to navigate.

For a variety of reasons the prep-boys started to change shifts. This meant we all worked together at various times and the concept of supervisors and supervised no longer existed. When I worked with Rick I always found it interesting although rarely enjoyable because he was constantly so negative.

He was a hangover from the Beat Generation, the Dionysian predecessors of the hippie movement. Their philosophy was that the only rule is that was there are no rules. While plenty of illegal pot was smoked, their drug of choice was LSD, which at that time was not illegal. Rick was never one to drop names, yet it was apparent he moved in circles which included counter-culture icons such as Jack Kerouac and Allen Ginsberg.

Between shows the two of us would decide who was going to prepare each stunt and then get the vessels ready to lay out when it was time to re-set the stage. When there was nothing to be done, Rick would sometimes tear off a piece of cardboard box and start writing on it with a stubby pencil. When asked what he was doing, he would reply that he was drafting the script for his next film. Somehow this did not fit my image of writers like Dickens or Kipling.

What Rick produced was described by him and everyone else as Underground films. This meant they were shot in 16mm black and white on an extremely low budget. None of the actors were paid, as most of them were friends and acquaintances, and Rick as director, made up a lot of the action as he went along.

His films all seemed to have crude and suggestive titles such as "Dry Hole", which had absolutely nothing to do with drilling for oil. Viewing one of his films in Greenwich Village, I later calculated having laughed three times at most and was totally bored for 58 of the 60 minutes un-edited running time. This counterculture stuff seemed ridiculous to me.

Rick referred to himself as an "ardist" and "rider", somehow transposing the "Ts" with a "D." One time, when we were just chatting, Rick made some reference to oral sex. I was not particularly enthusiastic about the concept of cunnilingus and asked him if he did that.

'It doesn't form a part of my regular diet,' he replied, 'but occasionally I enjoy eating at the "Y". If only he had said it can be very erotic and give a woman enormous pleasure, but maybe he himself did not fully understand that. Like most men of his generation he considered the penis to be in "pole position" and most references to sex related only to male desires and satisfaction.

One evening after a couple of drinks in a beer bar, Frank and I decided to walk in Central Park. It was five minutes to midnight and two policemen in a patrol car shouted at us to get out because the Park was closed from midnight onwards.

Typical of Frank, as soon as the police car had gone he said, 'Let's sit on the grass,' and he lit a cigarette. We did this thinking we were well out of sight behind some bushes. Ten minutes later the same police car passed along the road below using a searchlight to scan the hillside. Although we sat motionless I was amazed when the police car drove quickly up the rough, grassy embankment directly to confront us. Without hesitation Frank said: 'Deny everything.'

Blinding us with the spotlight, the cop yelled. 'Didn't I tell you two to get out earlier?' Frank protested vehemently that the policeman must be mistaken. But of course the police are not stupid, and let us know as much in no uncertain terms. I was not used to this type of confrontation and felt lucky not to have been given a ticket or even taken to the police station.

We decided to have a cold drink and stumbled, somewhat dazed, into a downmarket soda parlour. Before we had even ordered pizza, one of the gang members in the parlour jeered at Frank, saying, 'Did you guys have a good time in the Park?'

We then realised we both had grass on our backs and the connotation of this. Frank coped easily with this kind of situation, but I was still in shock from my encounter with the police and further upset by the ridicule.

Homosexuality was a big issue in the USA at this time. For a start, homosexual acts were illegal and the police had no qualms about pursuing and sometimes entrapping gay men. There was a stigma to homosexuality, and the straight community - from Midwestern preachers to Californian students - were all in effect verbal gay-bashers.

Though at this time the word gay had not been adopted and terms such as faggot and queer led the multitude of derogatory terms.

There was definitely a divide between those who were straight and those who were gay, but in the arts including the theatre environment such as ours, there was a complete live-and-let-live attitude. After all, if you removed all non-heterosexual people from the arts they would be substantially diminished.

Frank, who was 26, seemed amazing to me. He had an enviable confidence and a bravado which ensured he came out of most encounters unscathed and cheerfully optimistic. It was with this perception of Frank, that on our return to his apartment I listened awestruck to his stories.

'I used to be heavily involved in hypnotism while studying psychology at University,' he said. 'Hypnotised loads of people, perhaps as many as 300. My speciality was to take people back through pre-birth to an earlier life. Used this technique on my cousin and he revealed that in an earlier life he had been killed during the Civil War. Even gave his name as Joseph Dukovsky.'

Frank went on in his convincing way to say he was sure that stories such as this, and vague descriptions of a floating existence after death, had been recorded regularly and were probably being investigated by secret government agencies.

A few days later I went to a party at the Queens apartment of one of the pavilion hosts. Although there was a shortage of girls I was flattered that Lana, one of the hostesses, showed an interest in me. She was good fun during the evening, then, only the following day I learned that she had already made a date to go out with Frank.

Now there was a situation in which both Lana and Frank wished to cancel their date and were thinking up excuses. Lana, who wanted date me instead, told Frank she was sick. Frank was planning to tell Lana he had to cancel because his father was coming into town, when in reality it was because his girlfriend, Yvette, was returning to New York unexpectedly.

Seeing this comedic situation I no longer scoffed at the petty intrigues of theatrical farces, understanding that such improbable situations do sometimes occur.

When working a shift with Aaron, a van arrived to unload boxes of chemicals. There was a number tattooed on the delivery man's forearm, a stark reminder that such markings had been put on Jews in concentration camps. Aaron was visibly upset by this and seemed absent-minded for the rest of the shift. Later, Bernie told me Aaron had lost many of his relatives in Auschwitz.

I was constantly busy working as many overtime shifts as I could, or socialising. Not conscious of it at the time, but now more gregarious than ever and living with an intensity never to be duplicated. Most important of all, I was shaking off the social straitjacket of my youth and relishing my new-found individuality.

How incredibly lucky I was to have stumbled into New York at the time of the Worlds' Fair and landed a job which had brought me into contact with so many interesting people.

One of my many new experiences included an invitation to a predominantly gay party in the Village. It was a farewell gathering for one of the demonstrators who had landed a film part in Australia. I was the only non-theatre person there, all of the others being in some way connected to show-business. There was a piano in the apartment and it seemed that all of them could play and sing.

Having drunk quite a lot, I got into the mood of the evening. I even thought it funny when one of the inebriated men, whom I quite liked, started to dance with me in a very sexual way, rubbing up against my thigh.

Two of the dancers pulled him off, good-naturedly admonishing him, saying, 'You know Paul doesn't swing that way.' Everyone, including me, just laughed off the situation.

Karl, one of the demonstrators turned up later with his artist "girlfriend," Beatrice. I had heard Frank refer to her as a "fag-hag" describing a woman who enjoyed a non-threatening, easygoing relationship with gay men. Beatrice took an interest in me as the only straight man there and an easy target in my "relaxed" state.

It was only the next day I realised I had made a date with her, or she had made a date with me - couldn't quite remember the exact details. But - oh dear! I also remembered she was not very attractive.

Anyway, I set off once again for the Village, thinking it would be an experience if nothing else to have a date with this creative, somewhat different woman.

Her apartment was strewn with her "art nouveau" style paintings, which I have to say I really liked. She showed me her reproduction paintings of famous artists including, Gustav Klimt and Alphonse Mucha, which apparently sold well in the gay community.

A combination of genuine interest in her art and the free-flowing Chianti poured from a raffia-clad bottle led me to see her differently. She mellowed, slowly losing her tough New-Yorker persona to become softer, even sensual.

Through the course of the evening it became apparent that life in general, and men in particular, had treated her badly. She was basically an unhappy, disillusioned person carrying more than her fair share of emotional burdens.

'Fucked-up,' was Rick's brief summation when I told him about her. Just like everyone else in the Village, I thought, and although I liked her, one evening with Beatrice was enough for me.

I was hardly in a position to be critical of other people's hang-ups as my own thinking was riddled with illogical and conflicting concepts. At one party I was shocked by the overt sexuality of two young hostesses.

Or was it that I was shocked they were getting it on with a couple of married actors? Or was it the fact that the actors were older that really upset me? Or was it that I was simply jealous that I was not receiving the girls' attention?

At a time when I was trying to figure out and understand my own emotions and sexual drive how could I be so critical of others who were doing exactly the same? As if to add to my confusion a telling incident occurred when I and a group went to Central Park for a picnic. One of the demonstrators, Chris, a good-looking, athletic man of about 40, was there with his well-matched attractive actress wife.

After a few drinks sitting around in a circle joking, Chris reached across in front of me and playfully squeezed his wife's breast. Turning to me he said, 'Would you like to do that?' To which I replied that I would very much like to do that.

'Then you have my full permission to do so,' he said. I just laughed, until the question was repeated and it became apparent that this was a serious offer - a challenge. I looked directly at the actress who was of course the owner of the breast in question.

But as she gave no signal to either encourage or discourage me I became flustered and blushed. If only I could be rid of the guilt and embarrassment I suffered from anything relating to sex. If only I could be witty enough to defuse such situations.

Despite the good-natured teasing I really liked Chris. It seemed to me that he had all the right qualities, such as charm and good looks, to become a famous actor. Yet he like most performers had an obvious streak of narcissism.

It reminded me of something said by the wife of an extremely vain actor at the time of their divorce. 'The problem was,' she said, 'we were both in love with the same man.'

Chatting with Chris he made the point that it was really easy being a demonstrator. 'You don't need to have studied Lee Strasberg Method Acting for this,' he joked. Only one of the three men on stage had a speaking part while the other two merely went through the routine.

That gave me the idea that I could possibly move up the theatrical (and financial) ladder: so went to see the man whom everyone referred to as Walt, but I still called Mr. Schneider.

He seemed surprised that I should be interested in this job and perhaps also by my nerve in asking. He did not dismiss the request out of hand but merely said something about the requirement to obtain an actors' union card.

John, one of the people from the ship, had been given a phoney telephone credit card number and had not only used it himself but passed the number on to other people. Now the telephone company had traced some of his calls and he was hoping they would only send him a bill and not charge him with anything criminal.

After this had come to light, Jim worryingly phoned me from San Francisco, using the illegal number - but it was nevertheless good to hear his news.

Telephone handsets could not be purchased; they were the property of the telephone company who rented them. As the rental of a handset added to the cost of having one or more phones in a home, they themselves became items of value.

More as a status symbol than as a practical requirement, Frank had two telephones in his tiny studio apartment. Apparently the easiest place to "acquire" these was from the telephone booths in a hotel. Frank's had both come from the Waldorf Astoria. 'All you need is a good pair of scissors,' he said. 'But you do need to be sure they have a long enough lead attached or they are of no use.'

I saw quite a lot of Lana, the girl I had met at a party, the one who triggered a sort of theatrical farce. Mostly we enjoyed driving her compact convertible with the top down to one of the beaches or to the Village.

As if ticking off the list places about which I had heard, we made a trip to Coney Island. I do not know what I had expected but was seriously disappointed in this rundown, clearly working-class dump. More Blackpool than Bondi!

One weekend, when her parents were away Lana picked me up after work and drove me to her home in New Jersey, saying she would cook dinner. On arrival we found her younger sister and several of her high school friends were recovering from what looked like a three-day party.

Set in a beautiful area in which every lawn had been manicured to perfection, the house was expensively furnished with deep pile carpets. A white grand piano sat somewhat forlornly in a bay window at one end of the cavernous living room.

Later we went out for a drive in Lana's mother's outrageously flashy 1963 Olds Starfire. With the sheer muscle of its growling 6.4 litre V8 engine we repeatedly topped the magical "100." It wasn't so much that I could drive the car that fast - more like having to hold it back - restrain it like a powerful Dobermann on a leash.

Back at the house Lana poured three industrial measure glasses of gin and tonic. They must have been about half a pint each. The result was I fell asleep on the living room sofa long before dinner; probably not what she had in mind.

The following day she decided the two of us should go to her parents' country club for lunch. On arrival, without making eye contact or giving even the faintest glimmer of recognition, Lana tossed her keys in the direction of a "car-jockey," a very rude gesture even in America.

Nonchalantly she ordered drinks and food, regardless of whether she actually wanted them. My food and drink consumption was deliberately modest in an effort to minimize the bill. At one point, becoming concerned I might not have enough cash to pay, I surreptitiously counted the notes in my pocket.

It came as a great relief when Lana casually mentioned it was not possible to pay for anything in the club. She would have to sign for anything we wanted, just as she always did.

I was thinking more and more about Lana. Fascinated by this lovely sweet, outgoing and thoroughly spoilt child of 19. She appeared never to have faced any type of hardship or actually had to do anything she did not wish to.

The following Monday, working the late shift, we met in an isolated corridor just as the Pavilion was quieting down towards the end of the last show. Without hesitation we got into a heavy clinch, only to be startled by the opening of an outside door beside us. We both jumped about three feet, but fortunately it was only Gail, a rather prudish hostess who gave us a disapproving look before walking on.

I remember that day for an entirely different reason. It was when the Civil Rights Bill passed through the Senate: a reminder that slavery in America lay in the comparatively recent past. Jaydon, had by this time developed a sense of trust in me, finding it useful to speak with an unbiased non-American.

At quiet times he would talk about the constant and appalling abuse to which he as a young black man was subjected. The verbal insults, the derogatory names, the physical pushing. As bad were the silent, unintentional insults; people would look through him and talk over him as if he did not exist.

White people would refer to him as if he was mentally deficient, and of course there was the perpetual police harassment.

It made me aware of how lucky I was never to have been the object of prejudice. My only experience was of unarmed, benign British "Bobbies," predominantly like the popular 1960s TV series, jovial "Dixon of Dock Green" types who maintained order while at the same time enjoying the respect of most people they encountered.

Two days later there was an air of excitement and anticipation around the entire showground because a former American Vice-President was due to visit. Many of the Pavilion staff lined up outside to watch him pass. Hoards of visitors were also waiting to see this VIP.

For some reason, one group kept looking at me and pointing me out. Admittedly, I was wearing my rather embarrassing red jumpsuit, but as Bernie was there as well and similarly attired, I was confused. Then one of the tourists came up to me and asked if I was Swedish.

'No,' I said, 'I am from England.' The tourist returned to his Swedish group, whom it appeared had been ready to embrace me as one of their own, and I heard him pronounce 'Englander.' They were probably not too disappointed, assuming that this lanky, fair- haired young man was a throwback to some Viking invasion.

Then, former Vice President Richard Nixon arrived on foot, pressing the flesh with as many people as he could. He was shaking my hand when Bernie shouted out, 'He can't vote for you, he's English.' Nixon laughed but wasted no further time and quickly moved on.

The following day I was not due to work and surprisingly had no plans. Making my way to Central Park I sat on a bench soaking up the spring sunshine and enjoying the spectacular cherry blossom display.

At a nearby bench another man had been enjoying the same emotions and before quietly moving off philosophically said. 'In Japan, they welcome and acknowledge cherry blossom for its beauty. It is, they say a reminder that our lives are both precious and short.'

Then I mused about how much had happened since I left England. How the boredom and isolation of being "on-the-road" had given way to daily involvement with so many interesting people.

I was so lucky to have found not just a good job but to be immersed in such an enjoyable environment, surrounded by young people and having fun. Yes, having real, uninhibited fun for the first time in my life. There were no rules here, no boundaries and no ever-critical mother.

Coming to America with very little money was a gamble that had paid off. My job was secure for the next few months but what would I do when it came to an end?

Travel around the United States perhaps? Try to get to the Far East or even complete my westerly journey and circumnavigate the world all the way back to England? The specifics were vague; what was important was the need to save money so I could continue to travel.

A few days after Nixon's visit to the Fair, Lana and I went to a drive-in movie, colloquially referred to by

Sandy as a passion pit or finger bowl. It was indeed an experience to see hundreds of cars with a double-headed occupant in each: no one actually watching the movie. Beer bottles chinked, car doors slammed and the hamburger stall filled the air with charcoal smoke.

It must have been about 2 A.M. when we decided to leave. Many of the couples had already left but seeing people slumped in the cars made me understand the title of an Everly Brothers song, "Wake-Up Susie - Susie Wake-Up!"

Sandy, one of our transient sofa-occupying roommates, hailed from somewhere in the rural deep South. He came from a hick town called Hundschmit - or Dogshit as he preferred to call it. He said he once woke up in a drive-in at 5 A.M. after a rough night and a bad movie.

In the Bible Belt where he lived, he said there was a theme regularly regurgitated about pre-marital sex. One pastor said, 'Sex is dirty and disgusting' and in the next breath, 'You must save it for the person you love.'

He made people laugh as much because of his glacially slow southern drawl, as what he actually said. He referred to himself as a PK (preacher's kid) who wore Jesus boots (sandals) and seemed inordinately proud of the fact that he, and all the other shit-kickers (farm boys) had acquired the dubious skill of manufacturing E (explosives) out of fertiliser.

Having said that, the ability to improvise with explosives may well have proved useful to many of these young men, some of whom had already been drafted into the army.

Sandy was still enrolled in college which protected him from the draft, for the time being. He joked it might be necessary to study to Ph.D. level simply to stay alive.

Although the pavilion operated every day, Friday nights were still the big party night. After working the late shift, we went off to yet another party, this time in Queens. Bernie was driving Aaron's car and asked for a puff of his cigarette. They then offered it to me, but realising it was a reefer I declined. Mostly I was concerned and saddened that Aaron was finding dope to be increasingly necessary not just as a prerequisite for social events but for life in general.

This particular Friday the party was hosted by Travis Stevens, an electrician who specialized in theatrical work. He was a union man who seemed to work double shifts every day of the week and boasted he earned twice as much in a day as the prep boys earned in two weeks.

Understandably, Travis was permanently tired, although the joke was that because he was married to a Playboy bunny he didn't get much rest even when he was at home. Travis' idea of good hospitality was to have everybody drinking vodka or rum through straws out of watermelons. Bernie, looking in the direction of the Playboy bunny made some reference to Travis' pre-occupation with melons.

For some reason Lana left the party early, saying she was coming back - but she never did. I assumed this was because she was tired. The following night she did not show up for a party at my apartment which was in part, to celebrate her 20th birthday. That gave me the signal that her interest in me was waning.

The party was a great success with lots of interesting people arriving. Because of Lana's absence I did not enjoy myself as much as everyone else. I was genuinely confused not knowing if I really wanted her or if it was just that my ego was bruised.

As consolation I snogged a black girl for the first time. Enjoying her plump lips I was quite getting into it until she suggested we should tone it down a bit because, unknown to me, she was married and her husband was in the next room.

As the days passed I was still not sure whether the Lana saga was over. I did not know if she was playing games with me or had become bored and was moving on. In either case I was not too upset and even enjoyed the sense of freedom to cast my eye over the open field.

Out of the blue, Wen phoned and asked if she could come for the weekend. Surprised I happily agreed, but was annoyed when 24 hours later, she cancelled the visit. If nothing else, I was learning to go with the flow, to enjoy what could be enjoyed and not getting too upset when the boat rocked.

I was starting to feel that one either enjoys life or feels miserable depending on one's own attitude towards things. I determined to find the best in everything and to mix with people who gave me the biggest lift.

I was still in thrall to Frank, a man whom I saw as having succeeded in all life's great requirements. He was confident, outgoing, overtly sexual and totally at ease with the person he was. Our friendship was never forced but grew stronger.

We spent time together going out as a foursome with Yvette and Dagmar. We would go to "art-house" movies such as Francois Truffault's "Jules et Jim" the story of a ménage a trois set in the most atmospheric quarter of Paris. A story in which the two men's friendship was tested when they found themselves in opposing armies during the First World War.

Dreamily, I imagined myself as the brooding Oskar

Werner alternating between the happy relationship with the other man and their shared, melancholic love of the coolly seductive Jeanne Moreau.

It reminded me of the quip about the London Bloomsbury set of artists who were said to, "live in squares, paint in circles and love in triangles."

Frank visited a theatrical supply store where he acquired a sufficiently credible looking human head. This he placed in a draw on stage which the demonstrators opened during the show in order to take out a piece of equipment. Under the low lighting and with a liberal application of theatrical blood it appeared realistic.

It certainly had the desired effect with one of the demonstrators who in the middle of a show, quite literally screamed and jumped back in horror. The audience of course remained mystified by the peculiar behaviour onstage.

Some nights the Manhattan heat and humidity was so energy-sapping that I would flee the oppressive heat of the airless apartment and go to one of the Times Square all-night cinemas. The films were always ridiculous but the air conditioning did make the price of admission worthwhile. It seemed that I and the rest of the audience were all there to sleep through the rolling, triple-bill program.

When going to mainstream films in proper cinemas I was surprised to see hard-boiled New Yorkers cheering when the hero was successful and uninhibitedly weeping at the sad bits. The same people who could be so rude to another human being on a subway platform.

The more time I spent with Dagmar the more I liked and admired her. She was pretty, cheerful and completely unpretentious. She worked for a fashion magazine but was not herself overly immersed in fashion. I would like to have dated her properly but knew that she had a boyfriend whom she had been with through college.

That was until Frank mentioned Dagmar would like to go out with me. The implication being that she was interested in something more than merely going out in a group. Responding to my query he said the relationship with her boyfriend was now over. So without delay I made a date to take Dagmar to the Banjo bar.

Collecting her from the apartment I was bowled over by the transformation. The formerly mousy, auburn hair was now a dark ginger, cut in a modern, androgynous pageboy style. She was wearing a straight, lambs-wool sweater dress with a large belt which accentuated her slim waist.

Already knowing each other quite well we were relaxed in each other's company and the combination of beer and upbeat banjo music put us in a good mood.

Returning to Dagmar's flat we did not go in. Instead we lingered outside her door and kissed in a wonderfully affectionate and loving way. For both of us this had been a magical evening - for both of us there was the promise of something special to come.

When I got home I could not stop myself from telling Freddie all about Dagmar and how wonderful she was. Finally even the long-suffering Freddie could take it no longer and making some comment about a lovesick-limey, staggered off to bed.

The following evening, returning to the flat after the late shift, I found Wen had arrived without notice. Something, or more likely someone, had upset her badly and she needed comfort and support. I realised that her life was not happy but I was not mature enough to understand or confident enough to enquire about the underlying causes.

The straitlaced Freddie got quite a shock in the morning when he walked past my alcove and saw Wen in bed with me. In typical Freddie style, there was a lot of disapproving raising of eyebrows and loud sucking in of breath.

He simply could not understand how I could be in the process of falling in love with one woman and share my bed with another. I myself was a little confused by this but knew when Wen started to sob she needed a special form of comfort and reassurance: she needed to be held.

As if by divine retribution, Dagmar told me that her former fiancé was coming into town and wanted to see her. She assured me she had no intention of rekindling the relationship and that from now on only wanted only to be with me.

The boyfriend did come into town and painful though it was, I left them to finalise things. Much as I would like to have asked, I never enquired as to whether or not they had had "one for the road."

Accompanying the chemical stunt show in the Red Room was a five piece band. The musicians were all black except for the ultra-cool percussionist who spent most of his spare time practising.

In particular, using his vibraphone he repeatedly played the laid-back, exotic bossa nova hit song, "The Girl from Ipanema."

He had formed a relationship with a somewhat older not exactly beautiful but very sensual, Italian woman. I thought their lovemaking must be incredibly passionate and wondered if the ability to be rhythmic made musicians especially good lovers.

Between shows I would often chat with the laid-back musicians. They obviously saw and heard everything that went on but kept it to themselves, and other than being friendly, did not socialise. They were professional session players well beyond the age of most of the people working there.

The bass player, Calvin, was a particularly friendly chap and it was to him that I often gravitated. On one occasion I was holding the double bass, idly plucking the strings just before the next show was due to start.

Calvin walked away laughing - leaving me holding the base when the band struck up. Quite whether that qualified me to claim I had played music professionally I did not know.

On the weekend that Dagmar was sorting things out with her former boyfriend, Calvin invited me to go to a club and hear what he described as, 'some real cool jazz.' Without hesitation I accepted and we ended up at Club Harlem on 145th Street.

A relatively unknown (to me at any rate) musician called Oscar Peterson was playing. Through the course of the evening he dedicated a number to 'The Englishman we have here with us tonight' and sang, "A Foggy day in London Town."

Calvin was among friends and when the band took a break one of the musicians approached him and chatted briefly. Next thing I knew Calvin was onstage plucking the double bass. What amazed and delighted me was how melodic and tuneful the instrument sounded. A far cry from the boring background beat I was used to hearing at the chemical show.

After a while a female singer stepped onto the stage. Calvin had obviously worked with her before. Without discussion he started a wonderful riff on the base and after a few minutes she joined in with a song made famous by Ella Fitzgerald, "Tain't What You Do - Its the Way That You Do It."

It all sounded so mellow and hypnotic to me but Calvin was sure that two, maybe even three keys on the piano were not working properly. I was drawn in and seduced by everyone's friendliness and immersed myself in the rhythms and the ambience. It wasn't until the following day it dawned on me, that I a young 'honky', had been driving around Harlem at 2 A.M. with two black men.

It reaffirmed my belief that racism or indeed most forms of social segregation, had got it all wrong. If you like people and get on well it doesn't matter what colour skin you have or they have. By the same token we can dislike people who are ethnically and socially the same as us.

Another relevant factor is how much time and in what specific circumstances we overlap with someone. It may be fun to mix socially with some people but we would not necessarily be at ease living in close proximity to them. Moreover, I had already learned that we can enjoy some people's company without automatically liking their friends.

Chapter 6

DISASTER

Then disaster struck. I did something unforgivably stupid and it was entirely my fault.

During the performances we remained backstage preparing everything for a quick changeover for the next show. With half-an-ear as to what was going on we knew where they were in the routine, and how well it was going. Whether the demonstrators were getting applause in the right places, and were especially attentive to the drum-roll building up to the count of ten for the iodine clock to turn black.

This time the drum roll went on too long and it was obvious to me and the demonstrators that nothing was going to happen. Finally the lead demonstrator said to the audience, 'You just can't get decent help these days, and after a little sympathetic audience laughter, carried on with the show.

I felt absolutely terrible. It was my fault and I knew it. I had been careless; thinking about which bar we would go to that night and preparing all the demonstrations on autopilot.

Used correctly the basic ingredients for the clock were all relatively common and harmless. Boiling water, three per cent hydrogen peroxide, ascorbic acid, ten per cent iodine and cornstarch. But it was necessary to mix them carefully, and for a sufficient length of time. That is what I had failed to do.

It was embarrassing for the demonstrators and it had happened twice before with me and a few times with other prep teams. On this occasion it happened with a nervous young assistant called Beau. He lived in a perpetual state of agitation and was critical even when things were going well.

As soon as the show was over, he stormed backstage yelling...

'Which one of you fucking idiots screwed up this time? Oh, you! - no wonder the stupid fucking Englishman and the...'

'Leave Jaydon out of this,' I said before he could complete his racial slur. 'I prepared this demonstration and I'm really sorry it failed... I don't know why but I am really sorry.'

Beau was now inches from my face, screaming: 'You're not only arrogant you're a fucking incompetent dickhead. Whoever let a useless arsehole like you into the country?'

'You son of a bitch, you're a conceited fucking retard... you're incapable of doing your job.'

After another minute of this off-the-Richter-scale splenetic rage he was shrieking abuse so close to me that I could feel his spittle on my face. I too then became as unhinged and out-of-control as he was. Something in me snapped and I shouted,

'Fuck off you prick.' Reacting in the heat of the moment I swung my left hand out and punched him on the cheek.

I felt sure I would be sacked, especially as the man I had hit was gay. Beau meanwhile started rushing all over the place noisily complaining to everyone he could find.

It wasn't long before Walter Schneider appeared

and tried to restore calm. Beau kept shouting he was going to resign, until that is it became apparent that the thought of his departure did not appear to upset anyone.

Mr. Schneider was remarkably unruffled and fair in his handling of the whole situation. Perhaps this experienced theatre man, familiar with the mercurial nature of actors and the emotional pressures of performance could slip chameleon-like into the role of calm adjudicator.

The outcome was that both Beau and I were to take indefinite leave until the matter was resolved. I went straight round to Frank's apartment and told him what had happened. Frank's reaction was a shriek of laughter and massive congratulations.

'But why did you only give him a puny left hook when you are right-handed? He asked. 'Well perhaps fortunately for both of us,' I said, 'I was holding an Erlenmeyer flask in my right hand.'

Frank went on to say there were a lot of people in the pavilion who would like to have taken a swing at Beau. While this did cheer me up it did not alter the fact that in all likelihood I was now about to lose my very special job.

Dagmar's initial reaction was surprise; it seemed so out of character that this apparently well-mannered Englishman had resorted to this sort of bar-room-brawl behaviour. She too was aware that in all likelihood I would now be laid off. In sadness she commiserated with me but must also have wondered if there was some formally unseen, darker side to my personality.

A couple of nights earlier, Frank had met a girl who worked in a much smaller pavilion run by a brand-name ladies' hair colouring company. She had mentioned in general conversation that one of their hosts quit suddenly after receiving his draft papers and they were now urgently looking for a replacement.

I was outside the hair-colouring pavilion before it opened the following day. Smartly dressed, well groomed and following Frank's advice displaying chutzpah, I strode in with confidence and a smile.

It worked and I was taken on then-and-there by the all female management team. The three women responsible for hiring had come in individually to interview me. Well, what they actually did was come in and inspect me.

My English manners such as standing when they entered the room, together with my accent undoubtedly helped. They made me fill in some paperwork, fitted me out with one of their blazers, and told me to return later in the day for on-the-job training. The salary was $80 per week with the opportunity to work overtime.

I met the other hosts on the daytime shift. They were all tall, attractive men but by no means clones. Theophilus as his name implied, was of Greek extraction and he had a sensual, languid, Mediterranean manner about him. Sven was a stereotypical Nordic blond with watery blue eyes. Chuck the Iowa farm boy, was a college football quarterback who looked and acted the part to perfection.

I began to realise that I had not been hired for my Mensa-level IQ. I had been hired as a sort of non-sexual gigolo whose English accent would amuse the women waiting to get in. Sometimes I even heard women in the line-up discussing the relative attributes of the hosts. One woman loudly exclaimed to her friend that she would like to get her hands on Chuck's rock hard buns.

The other men and I were mere pieces of meat

on display. For the first time I realised what girls and women endured much of the time in a world of boorish, chauvinistic men.

It was the end of my second working day in the girls' playpen when I received a message to drop in and see Mr. Schneider. I was greeted warmly which surprised me as I assumed I was about to be formally fired. Instead he said I could resume work first thing in the morning. Beau would also be returning to work that day and it was hoped that there would be no further friction.

It turned out Rick had been highly supportive of me, telling Mr. Schneider that Beau was considered to be obnoxious by most people and it was he who had initiated the dispute. Well, actually what Rick said was, 'Beau was a snivelling little douche bag and it was amazing no one had taken a poke at him before.'

Now I had a dilemma: technically being employed by two companies I was a latter-day Servant of Two Masters. Considering the possibility of holding down two jobs simultaneously I realised that it would not be possible to dovetail unpredictable shifts.

Coming to my senses I determined instead to be the most reliable chemical mix man on the planet. Phoning the hair colouring company I apologised and said I was unable to continue for undisclosed "personal" reasons. She slammed down the phone and "forgot" to pay me for the two days I had worked.

Okay, that's fair enough I thought. It was no different than paying for an insurance policy you are pleased never to use.

When Beau and I passed in a narrow backstage corridor, I approached with my hand outstretched and apologised. Beau, who had not of course been to school in England and therefore did not play by the same rules, avoided eye contact and brushed past.

Had there been any lip-readers in the vicinity they might have been able to interpret his murmured phrase which sounded somewhat like, 'Fuck you.'

Any thoughts I might have had about joining the demonstrators onstage was now clearly never going to happen. But amazingly, work in the pavilion and in my social life continued more or less unchanged.

Well, there was some change and it was all for the better. Dagmar and I spent as much time together as we could. Going to parties and our favourite bars such as the Cave des Moines and The Red Onion. She showed me how to have fun and how to be less serious as we laughed uninhibitedly, danced to the upbeat music and became lost in our own private world.

Most of the pavilions employed hosting staff, predominantly students working through the summer vacation. As they circulated around the pavilions they only had to show their pass in order to get admission without having to line up.

One evening we watched the House of Japan show from the projection booth before going on to the Singer pavilion. A host from the Singer pavilion, aware of the vast numbers of pretty girls working with us, arranged a vacuum cleaner demonstration, presumably as a sort of metaphorical foot-in-the-door.

Between shows he spread a large amount of sand across the floor in the centre of the Red room only to discover that the cord on his vacuum cleaner was too short to reach any of the electrical sockets. We all laughed but for some reason he failed to find it amusing. It could have had something to do with the fact the hostesses he had intended to impress were hastily dispatched to find a dustpan and brush.

A letter arrived from my father with some unexpected news. He had accepted an offer to work in Bermuda. I was pleased he had received a promotion and would have the excitement of living somewhere different and beautiful. It also meant that I no longer had a home in England. This did not worry me as I never intended to live with my parents again but it was a bit strange to feel my sea anchor had been torn away.

Time was starting to run out and there were only two more months before the Fair closed. Understandably things became more casual and relaxed as the visitor numbers dwindled. Bernie the extrovert, frustrated 'would-be' actor, was always thinking up wacky stunts which usually allowed his appearance on the stage.

One part of the show involved darkening the stage prior to a demonstration of chemiluminescence, a process in which light was created chemically. This is where Bernie would sometimes bizarrely drift across the stage carrying a lit candelabra. No-one knew what he was trying to do but it may have had some connection with Phantom of the Opera.

Once or twice Bernie managed to persuade me to join in but I was always careful to interrupt only on occasions when I knew those demonstrators liked me and would welcome a break from their routine.

In the side theatre dance show there was an energetic number, the finale of which had the female dancers rushing into the wings. As a joke an imposing black male dancer stood in the wings, buck-naked with one foot raised on a chair. All the female dancers were worldly-wise and un-shockable.

Except one who was uncharacteristically prissy, and

as planned it was she who exited the wings at such speed she practically wrapped herself around this man. Screaming loudly she quickly complained to Mr. Schneider who by this time was probably beyond caring about the shenanigans of his recalcitrant children.

On the subject of children, I was surprised to learn that Walter Schneider was not only married but had two children. He was married to a theatrical set designer. The story was that she was lesbian but they both wanted children and this was their solution.

Whether or not they actually "did it" or used a turkey-baster was the subject of some speculation.

Steve, one of the hosts, was a film student and would hold film parties in his apartment. On a borrowed 16mm projector he showed silent black and white classics. Films such as Nosferatu, the 1922 adaptation of Bram Stoker's work in which Dracula now became Count Orlok. Compellingly horrific is the famous scene of a tall, thin menacing silhouette descending a stone staircase.

After having seen a couple of movies in the horror genre Dagmar and I were not planning to go again. Fortunately we did go one more time and saw the 1925 Sergei Eisenstein film Battleship Potemkin. This was probably the greatest propaganda film ever made, but also a genuine work of art.

The scene showing civilians being massacred on the Odessa Steps is breathtakingly awesome and powerfully shocking.

When, yet again, there was a vacancy in the apartment, we were contacted by a friend of a friend called Stan who seemed quiet and pleasant enough, and so he moved in. Two weeks later he and his belongings disappeared without notice, without him having paid any rent and without returning the keys.

Having lost some of my English reserve I went to the university department where Stan worked and challenged him in front of his work colleagues. Although cowed by this he turned out to be a gutless little creep who promised to pay the rent he owed, but in the end sent only a rude letter containing a few derisory dollars. I was all for pursuing the matter but Freddie urged me to tone down my aggression and suggested we should just forget the whole thing.

After advertising again for a roommate we received some really weird phone calls from men who often hedged around the question of homosexuality. I even had one man who sounded so much like a girl that I thought it was one.

It never even crossed my mind to find a female roommate. In those days, shared accommodation was never mixed. If a man and woman lived together it was assumed that they were in a sexual relationship and this in turn was also frowned upon.

Before leaving England I had been optimistic about the opportunity to form new friendships and was vaguely aware that I might encounter people with whom I did not get on. What I never expected was to have to work with someone who formed an intense dislike of me. This man was Tab Steiner, one of the demonstrators, aged about 40, who described himself as an actor-comedian.

The bit about being a comedian always puzzled me as I had never heard him say anything funny, witnessed him belly-laugh or even smile. The closest he came to this was to sneer while emitting a self-satisfied snort. He produced a stream of belittling and withering remarks, which presumably he thought to be clever and funny, although they lacked the imagination and acerbic wit of Gore Vidal, the master of that particular genre.

It turned out Tab's nightclub comedy routine, mostly practised in the Borscht Belt Jewish resort area in the Catskill Mountains, was based on finding a patsy in the audience and publicly taunting and humiliating him. The majority of the audience then becoming dishonourably complicit in sacrificing a fellow patron in order to protect themselves from falling prey.

By this time I realised that being gay no more defined a man's personality than does heterosexuality. Just as heterosexual men can range from assertive to passive, pleasant to undesirable, so can gay men. Tab worked very hard at being aggressive and unpleasant, ensuring that the way he acted and dressed gave no hint of his sexual orientation.

Quite why he took such an intense dislike to me I did not understand. Yes, there had been the occasional failure of an experiment, but that had happened with other demonstrators and other prep teams. This was something more intense, more personal.

Despite the prevalence of homosexuality in New York, especially in theatrical and artistic circles, its practice was not only illegal but disapproved of by the majority of straight society. I had made the over-simplified assumption that there was a bond between all gay men. But I did notice Tab never attended any of the parties, including those hosted by and predominantly for gay men.

At the end of one such party I and Dominic, whose apartment it was, were the only people remaining. Resting on the coffee table was a cereal bowl full of multicoloured pills and capsules. He offered them to me and laughed when I declined, revealing they were only outdated medicines put there for effect.

'But I can provide something more interesting if you would like me to?' he enquired. Both of us were pretty drunk at this time. Feeling at ease I asked why Tab was so obnoxious to me.

'Well,' said Dominic, 'Tab has never achieved any real success. Like all actors he had a theatrical biography listing his credits but it was obvious to everyone it was no more than a purse padded out with pennies. Tab has just passed his 41st birthday. He is starting to accept that the fame and recognition he sought is unlikely to be achieved. And like all of us he yearns for love but has to make do with mere encounters.

'You are an uncomfortable reminder to him of youthful potential. You are half his age, attractive and still have your whole life ahead of you. He has seen you having fun, laughing and mixing easily. Gifts he both envies and despises.'

One of Tab's favourite tricks to diminish me was to refer to me as female. Knowing that I was within earshot he would make comments such as, 'She's such a stupid bitch. Thank goodness the Vietnam war is likely to remove her from the gene pool.'

As intended, I became upset and flustered in these situations, either pretending not to have heard or stammering an inadequate response. It was Rick who gave wise counsel, telling me that my displays of embarrassment were exactly what Tab wanted.

'Chill out man,' was his advice: 'learn not to be drawn into other people's weirdness. Don't let scumbags like Beau or Tab control your actions.'

From then on I tried to be more careful and manage my responses to the unpleasantness. The jibes did not diminish but I had learnt a valuable lesson, it was not to respond in the way that Tab wanted me to: not to be manipulated by someone else but to choose my response in order to protect my sanity and maintain my morale. The very same morale which Tab was so intent on destroying.

Then I remembered something my school rugby coach was always saying. "Attack is the best method of defence." So the question became, how could I fire a broadside at Tab? I did not have the same ready wit and whatever I said merely seemed to confirm Tab's mastery over the situation.

The answer was presented a few days later when visiting Freddie during his nightshift at the photo library. Looking through the "secret file" we saw a picture of two, middle-aged women pulling their tops up to reveal saggy, pendulous breasts. It was Freddie who said that if we could get a picture of Tab, preferably with someone else, we could superimpose the heads replacing those of the two women.

The question became how to get a photograph of Tab? He would be very suspicious if any of the prep-men asked to take his picture. Although I was bursting with laughter at the very thought of this, I was careful with whom I shared the idea. If it leaked out, not only would Tab avoid having his picture taken but the element of surprise would be lost.

I did confide in Frank who thought the whole idea was hilarious. He suggested I should tell my friend Calvin, who was in a perfect position up there on the band dais, to take pictures of the people on stage.

The photographs Calvin took were perfect. On that day, Tab had been working with Beau and the pictures showed them both looking very smug and self-satisfied during the applause they received after successfully performing one of the chemical stunts. A stunt which incidentally, had been prepared for them by me.

There was a feeling Freddie never really had to

work too hard, especially on the night shift. That all changed when we processed Calvin's roll of film. The two men's faces had to be printed the same size as the two women's faces, then to be cut out carefully with an artist's scalpel and placed over the print of the two women before the whole thing was re-photographed and once again printed.

The result was sensational. I was cautious enough to take the mounted 8x10 print into work on a day when neither Tab nor Beau were due to work. First I showed it to the band who laughed hysterically. Then it was shown to a couple of the hosts and hostesses.

Within an hour, word had spread and everybody was coming to me wanting to see the picture. Even the actors and dancers, gay or straight, wanted to see it and all thought it very funny. One of them even left it in the green room from which I had to retrieve it despite this area technically being off-limits to the prep-boys.

The next day when Tab came in to work he tried his oily charm, saying he had heard about this amusing picture and wanted to see it. Always wary of this devious and unpredictable character I laughed, and obviously lying, claimed to have no knowledge of it. By this time I had ensured the incriminating evidence was safely away from the pavilion.

From then on I could not help but smile every time I saw Tab - and Tab, well aware of this, knew that the tables had been turned.

The pavilions operated from 10 A.M. until 10 P.M. with the fair-ground catering and entertainment establishments staying open much later. All employees entered the site via turnstiles after showing a guard their photo pass. I arrived for one afternoon shift having left my pass at home.

As I walked up to the turnstiles one of the black hostesses was just leaving. I borrowed her pass and entered without difficulty, thus proving that in those days security was neither efficient nor a particularly high priority.

The following day I was working the early shift and arrived at 9 A.M. just as the loudspeakers were playing the Star Spangled Banner. This was followed by an announcement that Winston Churchill was gravely ill.

I had taken to eating some meals at the reasonably priced cafeteria in the Pan Am building. There I formed an acquaintance with an English chap who, like me, had plans to travel further afield.

Harry's intention was to buy something like a Volkswagen camper van and drive down to South America. The more I heard about these plans the more enthusiastic I became about teaming up with him. At one point Bernie even said that he would like to come along with us to make a film about the whole expedition.

The idea of Bernie taking time out to travel was completely unrealistic. Despite having lived at home throughout the time he was working, and making exactly the same money as me, he had not saved anything.

There were other options to be considered. I could continue to travel westwards to South-East Asia and India, countries which held some inexplicable but magical appeal. Alternatively, I could remain in New York.

Dagmar and I had discussed the possibility of my staying in New York rather than travelling. There was some merit to this idea as it would have allowed our relationship to strengthen.

Perhaps subconsciously I was frightened this would

lead to marriage for which I was not ready. Anyway I thought, if I was ever to do some adventurous travelling this was surely the time for it.

Dagmar and I now found ourselves in an awkward situation. We had known each other and enjoyed each other's company for nearly six months. But only having been lovers for three months we were already facing the prospect of my departure in a few weeks.

This impending departure created mixed feelings for me. My vague and barely formulated long-term plan was to return to the United States and settle down in a proper job. Dagmar on the other hand had come out of a long-term relationship she thought was heading towards that all-important 1960s institution - marriage.

Now, the man she was genuinely fond of and who reciprocated that affection was for some inexplicable reason determined to go off travelling to a still undetermined destination for an unspecified period of time.

A few weeks before the show was due to end it was my 21st birthday. Dagmar and I planned to hold a party at the East 53rd Street apartment and everyone would be invited. Freddie used a duplicator to produce copies of the invitation which were distributed to all the prep-boys, hosts, actors and dancers.

The party was well attended, even by non- partygoers like Calvin, who had come simply to wish me all the best. The final seal of approval and confirmation that the function had been a success was the arrival of the police at 2 A.M.

The last few weeks of the fair felt quite different. There was steady routine but no pressure. The intense excitement had mellowed and everyone was looking towards their own future plans. Some of the hosts had already left in order to return to their colleges prior to the start of term.

On the final day there was certainly no sign of lethargy, everyone was hyped-up and excited. In the very last Red Room show I accomplished the seemingly impossible. Managing to crawl behind the set and manipulate the drawers from the rear, which caused them to mysteriously open and close at random during the show.

On a given signal I created such a commotion with the drawers that the demonstrator's attention was drawn to them. Bernie then stepped out and smashed a custard pie into Tab's face. The whole audience including Walter Schneider, who was mingling among them, roared with laughter.

If the show ended on a high note, the following week was depressing. Rick and I had to stay on for a while to clean the glass vessels and pack up chemicals. But gone were all the hosts and hostesses, gone was the band, gone were the dancers and demonstrators. Gone was all the vitality and swirling emotion.

During the next few nights I dreamt of the show and visualised mixing the chemicals and preparing the stunts. I was suffering a form of withdrawal due to the lack of hyper-stimulus.

Travis Stevens the macho electrician was still working around the pavilion disconnecting power and removing cables. His wife the Playboy bunny came in one day looking for him.

When she could not find him she sat on a packing case and chatted with me for a while. 'Travis and I are separating:' she said 'our marriage was a mistake.' She had not realised Travis was gay until after their whirlwind romance and Las Vegas wedding.

My relationship with Dagmar was not without tension either. It had nothing to do with the sex which was gentle and loving when we could find the privacy for it. The underlying cause was Dagmar's uncertainty as to where our relationship was going. This was put under far greater pressure when I received an ominous looking letter.

Chapter 7

THAT LETTER

The sword of Damocles, which hung over all young men in America at this time, had now fallen on me. The letter bore an official looking American government stamp around which was written "Selective Service System."

The large lettering at the top of the letter spelt out "ORDER TO REPORT FOR INDUCTION". The letter was formal and brief, notifying me that I had been reclassified 1-A and was legally required to report to Fort Bragg North Carolina, on a date, six weeks hence. A mere 42 days!

Attached to the letter was a rail travel pass and stuck to that by transparent tape was a dime. The purpose of this I never understood; was this the American equivalent of accepting the King's shilling, or more prosaically was it to phone the authorities on arrival at Fort Bragg?

Oh shit! To say panic ensued would be an understatement. I thought of myself as British with no moral obligation to join the American army let alone get sent to Vietnam. A war from which nearly 60,000 men with an average age of 23 would be returned to their families in body bags.

Jaydon had once said that after basic training, blacks and new immigrants would be the first to be sent to Vietnam. Just for good measure, Frank added that those same two categories were also the first ones to be sent into action. The reality was that almost every new recruit could expect to be sent to Vietnam relatively soon after completing a few weeks basic training.

Dagmar was totally distraught. The effect of this letter was going to impact her as seriously as me. 'Oh my poor darling. What are you going to do?' she said. That of course was the pivotal question. One thing was certain. I would not voluntarily go into the Army. The sample treatment I had received during my pre call-up medical was so distasteful I would avoid it if at all possible. That was before even considering the thousands of Viet Cong whose primary raison d'être would be to kill me.

In the endless discussion which followed this hammer blow Freddie raised an interesting question.

How was it that the Draft Board had the correct address for me? On arrival in the US I had given the YMCA as the place in which I would be staying. It was from that address that I was called by the Draft Board to undertake the medical examination. When I moved into the apartment with Freddie, I conveniently forgot to notify the Draft Board.

It could of course have been obtained through my pay and tax records, or there may have been a more sinister explanation. Invitations for my 21st birthday party with the address of my apartment had been widely circulated. Could it be that Tab, who as a gay man would never be drafted, had employed a practice used by many bearing a grudge and notified the Draft Board of my whereabouts?

It seemed paradoxical that being gay provided a legitimate "get out of jail" card as far as the Draft Board was concerned. The laws relating to homosexuality applied only to sexual acts not to orientation. So despite the opprobrium, it was not unknown for straight men to claim they were homosexual when dealing with the Draft Board.

Concerning the key question of stay or go, I knew from the moment I received the letter that I would leave. Discussion to the contrary was to soften the effect on Dagmar and assuage my guilt. A mere six weeks in which to act did have implications relating to what I would do next. Harry was not in any particular rush to drive to South America and had not even started to look for a vehicle. Another solution had to be found.

Prior to receipt of the draft letter, I had made tentative enquiries with an agency which matched vehicle owners who wanted to move cars across the country with drivers. This was done for a variety of reasons. Sometimes a family might just be moving to another part of the country and they either had more than one car or did not wish to drive.

There might also have been the opportunity to reduce State sales tax if the car was purchased in one state but registered in another. The most popular route for drivers was from New York City to San Francisco or LA and that is the route I wished to undertake. Because of this route's desirability I would have had to wait some weeks to get a car. Time I could not afford as my rendezvous at Fort Bragg was rapidly approaching.

So when offered the chance to take a car to Anchorage Alaska, which sounded different and exciting, I accepted. Studying my Mercator world map it looked as if there might even be some advantage in travelling from Alaska to the Far East.

During my last couple of weeks in New York City there were so many different emotions swirling through my mind. There was a sense of excitement about my next big journey but there was also the emptiness following the activity of the Pavilion.

Most importantly there was the heightened tension with Dagmar. For her, life went on routinely; she was in the same job and still had to go into work every day at the same time. She was genuinely attracted to and fond of me, but there was the underlying and unspoken reality that we would probably not have a long-term future together.

When we were out laughing, drinking and having fun she thought of me as an eccentric Englishman. When less upbeat, she thought of me as being peculiar and odd.

A man who appeared to be both very mature yet unbelievably naive. A man who acted so differently to all American men of the same age. That had been part of the attraction for her but was also part of the current problem. How was she to deal with this strange unpredictable character?

Fleeing from the Draft Board would banish me from the United States for the foreseeable future and quite possibly forever. Although never stated, the dilemma facing Dagmar was that at nearly twenty-three, she would be expected, by the prevailing American tradition, to be in a stable relationship with a slightly older man. This in turn would anticipate marriage and children.

I worked up to and including Wednesday October 28 and was due to collect the car in Brooklyn at 11.00A.M. on Friday, October 30. So, on the Wednesday Dagmar and I went to a couple of our favourite haunts, the Red Onion and the Night Court. We laughed and touched a lot but a careful observer would have detected tell-tale signs of underlying tension.

On my final night in New York, Frank, Yvette, Dagmar and I went out together. We started at a chain restaurant, Tad's Steakhouse which had always been a favourite of mine. They cooked the steaks right in the street window with fat-fuelled flames leaping high above the grill. There was nothing like that in England let alone in parochial little Seavale.

At the Night Court we drank beer and laughed, reminiscing about various incidents which had taken place over the last seven and a half months. No embarrassing story was left untold. So good of Frank and Yvette to keep our spirits raised. Mostly they needed to protect dear Dagmar for whom my departure seemed so unfair: almost like a form of amputation.

Frank and Yvette generously decided to spend the night in Frank's tiny studio flat so that Dagmar and I could enjoy the East 78th street apartment. Our final night together produced a swirling blend of love, lust and loss. Our lovemaking swung between intensity and tenderness, tears running down our cheeks blending into salty kisses.

Of course I enjoyed the sex but of equal value was the intimacy. That wonderful bond lovers create when they have just shared the intensity of passion. The release of physical and emotional inhibition, the unguarded revelation of our authentic self.

A wonderful experience that is so comparatively rare, so fleeting, so precious. An achingly beautiful emotion which cannot be artificially created or purchased by even the richest sultan.

Chapter 8

THE DRIVE

Arriving at the car Yard in Brooklyn I had no idea what make or model of car I would be given for the 4,700 mile drive to Alaska. I had heard of someone who had been given a small truck for the San Francisco run. Not very fast or glamorous but he was able to sleep in the back and use it as a sort of downmarket motor-home.

I was resigned to taking anything but was thrilled when it turned out to be a 1965 model Pontiac Catalina with only a few hundred miles on the clock.

This Yank-tank was a huge beast, encrusted in chrome and armed with a 389 cubic inch V8 engine which throbbed in a sensual, macho way. Conforming to the fashion of that model year, it had twin vertically-stacked headlamps and narrow whitewall tyres.

If there was one thing that disappointed me it was that despite the enormous overall size of this car, it was only a two door coupe. Moreover, the trunk and backseat were stuffed with the owner's belongings, which partially obscured my rear-view and in my opinion affected the handling of the car.

When I received "the letter" it had given me 42 days notice of the required date of Induction. There was now a countdown to what I referred to as the dreaded ID - Induction Day. Two weeks had been consumed making my decisions, finishing work at the Fair and finalising arrangements with the car company. Now setting off the clock was ticking down to ID-28.

Arriving at a non-descript hamlet in Pennsylvania at the end of the first day's drive, my eyes ached and I was totally exhausted. All I could think about was Dagmar and how much I missed her - wishing we could be together that night. It was especially ironic as I now had a motel room all to myself.

Next morning I started what was to become my routine, leaving at sunrise and driving for about an hour and a half before stopping for breakfast. The car had as much power as I could use and it was so sleek and beautiful even blasé gas station attendants commented on it.

This was a time in which each State set its own speed limits, usually around 75 mph on the turnpikes although a couple of states such as Montana and Nebraska had no speed limit at all.

While looking out for police, I cruised easily along the turnpikes at 85mph, and occasionally I saw the speed effortlessly rise to over 100. In the first few days I was especially conscious of my obligations if the car was to be involved in any kind of an accident. It would cost me personally a great deal of money, at least the $1000 deductible, and there would of course be substantial delays in a country I urgently needed to leave.

More importantly, the delay in my departure from New York while waiting for the car had brought me uncomfortably close to ID. Once this date passed I would legally be classed as a draft-dodger and deserter, liable for both imprisonment and enforced induction into the American army. Oh my God! What an appalling prospect.

In rural Wisconsin I drove past one isolated farm after another. Then I passed an enormous billboard promoting John Deere farm equipment. Emblazoned in large letters was the company slogan, 'We Stand Behind our Equipment.' Someone had scrawled across the bottom, 'Bet they don't stand behind their muck spreaders.'

Still chuckling at this I was speeding along fast approaching a yellow school bus which slowed down and stopped with its lights flashing. Thinking nothing of it I sailed past the bus. It was only when the driver sounded the horn loudly in an obviously irate manner I realised that in the US, drivers are not allowed to overtake school buses when their lights are flashing.

Worse still it dawned on me that children, used to being able to cross the road without the requirement to think for themselves could well have run in front of me. Understandably I slowed down and drove very sedately. About fifteen minutes later I could hear the wailing siren of a police car and saw in the rear-view mirror that it was closing on me. Had the school bus driver reported the incident and was this police car now after me? Whatever the situation there appeared to be no point in exacerbating the problem by speeding up.

Then I noticed a sign indicating that I had crossed the state border into Minnesota. Within minutes of passing the "Welcome to Minnesota" sign, the police car switched off its siren and receded out of sight. Was it all a coincidence, or had I just been extremely lucky? Prior to departure I purchased what I thought would be a useful book of maps. As my only experience of maps was a school Atlas, that is what I purchased. It was with the page showing the United States and Canada that I planned my route from New York City to Anchorage. Just following signs for the next major city en route.

As I made progress I used a pencil to mark my course on the Atlas, showing the date and place where

I stopped overnight. Proudly I wrote in my diary that this journey had taken me through lovely Pennsylvania, with its forests in glorious autumn colour and North Dakota's wonderful Painted Valley.

Entering Montana the car radio restricted me to a diet of country and western music. This should have come as no surprise as many people dressed like cowboys. I even saw one mounted rider in chaps and full cowboy regalia, only the six-gun was missing.

As if to compensate for this deficiency the ubiquitous pick-up trucks usually had a rifle slung across the rear window of the cab.

After a particularly long day's drive I crossed the border into Canada and felt relief at being temporarily out of the United States. Seeing a sign which read "Stay in the Train - Last motel for 15 miles," I stopped for the night. What surprised me was that the Train motel was exactly that: a collection of three or four 1930s railway sleeper carriages redolent of a bygone era.

Sitting in a coffee shop next day I overheard two farmers discussing the purchase and sale of land. 'Oh that farm is quite large,' said the first, 'it is seven quarters.' There were more references to farm sizes never mentioning acres or hectares; always quarters. When I asked about this I was told that most of southern Canada was nominally divided into square miles, 640 acres.

Homesteaders, the early settlers, were given a quarter square mile of land (160 acres) and from that time on farmers often referred to farm size by the number of quarters.

Throughout the American Midwest and the Canadian prairies the farms were usually isolated. Even visiting the nearest small town provided little opportunity to purchase anything other than the basics. So the rural population relied on the three-inch-thick Sears Roebuck catalogue for most of their needs.

One apocryphal story tells of a farmer writing to Sears saying, 'Send me one of them pumps on page 349. If it's any good I'll send you a cheque.' Sears replied, 'Send us a cheque and if it is any good we will send you a pump.'

Passing through Calgary I encountered the first snow. Driving northwards up the highway I saw numerous odd looking metal structures, the front of which moved slowly up and down. They were "nodding donkeys," the name used to describe the pumps which replace an oil rig after the well has been sunk.

Reaching Edmonton 180 miles further north I was driving through high winds and a full blizzard. At the city outskirts I saw shack-like, clapboard houses which appeared little better than those seen in cowboy films. I determined that the one place in the world I would never live was Edmonton.

Given that it was late in the day and because of the snowstorm I went into the centre of the city to find lodgings. I had learnt that buying a copy of the local paper gave me a feel for the place in which I was staying. In Edmonton I found a paper seller huddling inside the entrance to a pedestrian subway, sheltering from the biting wind.

The newspaper seller only said three words to me. 'Thank you, sir.' But the way in which he said them immediately caught my attention. He spoke with a very upper-class British accent. Taking a second look at the newspaper vendor I noticed he was predominantly dressed in fur.

A three-quarter length fur coat, knee-high fur boots and a fur hat pulled down over the ears. His clothes were obviously expensive but also incongruous in a city where most people wore heavy parkas and denim.

I tried to engage the man in further conversation and while his demeanour was civil and courteous, it was obvious that he either did not wish to communicate or for some reason was unable to.

Sitting in my room I thought more about the newspaper seller than the paper I had obtained from him. Clearly this man who spoke with "received pronunciation" came from an upper-class British family. But what was he doing in this isolated, chilly backwater? Selling newspapers would obviously not produce enough money to purchase his extravagant clothing.

Even the most affluent people in Edmonton would never wear such clothes, with the possible exception of the hat. My guess was that the newspaper seller probably had some form of learning disability.

Had he fled his home or had embarrassed parents dispatched him to this far-flung wilderness? Had a loving mother or caring relative purchased these apparently suitable clothes to keep him warm and assuage their guilt at banishing him?

Years later I met an effortlessly debonair Canadian businessman in London. The first thing that surprised me was how British he looked and sounded. He was dressed in a well-cut grey suit and once again spoke with an RP accent. When asked about his background he told me he had been born on Salt Spring Island off the coast of British Columbia.

Out of his wallet he took a sepia photograph of an ancient car with a deer strapped to the running board. 'This was my father on Salt Spring in about 1932. He was among the last of the remittance men.'

Going on he explained that from the late 1800s to the

early 1900s affluent British families found a way to rid themselves of dissolute and wayward younger sons. Those who had managed to disgrace themselves or had a propensity for drink and gambling were required to disappear far into unknown territory.

They in turn would have a regular income remitted to them: hence the name "remittance men". In the case of this Canadian businessman, he said an aunt had visited and insisted he should return to England to attend boarding school.

So had that poor newspaper vendor in Edmonton been a latter-day version of a remittance man?

Dawson Creek, British Columbia, is "mile zero" of the Alaska Highway, the supply route built by the Americans during the war. That meant the end of paved road with only gravel and potentially difficult conditions ahead.

Within 85 miles of Dawson that is exactly what I encountered: a blinding snowstorm which caused me to slide along the ice at a mere fifteen or twenty mph. While I may have lowered my speed it did not affect the enormous, juggernaut-like American trucks which came hurtling towards me.

Their turbulence buffeted the car and created a swirling vortex of gritty-snow which stung the car and reduced visibility to a guessing game.

Going round one icy left hand bend in the Rocky Mountains really scared me. The overly-heavy rear end caused the car to slide towards the edge of the road. I knew that counter-intuitively I had to steer into the skid, despite the fact that the car was drifting towards a steep drop into the valley below.

Petrified, I unfastened my lap-belt and was ready to jump out if the car went over. From then on I considered driving without fastening the lap-belt as a precautionary measure against a similar incident occurring again. In any case I was unsure as to the usefulness of lap-belts. Even my basic understanding of physics predicted that in the case of a head-on collision the human body would pivot at the waist, causing the torso to impale on the steering column and the head to smash onto the dashboard.

When I needed a break I would stop the car by the side of the road to stretch my legs and have a pee. If another vehicle happened to come along they would always slow down and without actually stopping, enquire courteously through the open window as to whether everything was alright. Given assurance there was no problem, they would touch the accelerator and with spinning wheels, slowly fish-tale off again.

Since leaving Dawson Creek I found myself to be an unofficial member of the Alaska Highway fraternity. Drivers on that road were always prepared to help others. So it was that I too slowed down and called through the window as I passed any vehicle which had stopped. I started to recognise and exchange a wave with other vehicles which were driving north.

Inevitably people would stop at different times and drive at different speeds, leapfrogging each other. These simple encounters were important, reminding me that I was part of the human race and not merely a lonely automaton whose only function was to steer a car.

I had acquired some much-needed new driving skills on the loose gravel and icy road, but just past the sign which read Alaska Highway Mile 820 I found conditions particularly difficult. After driving a further two miles I got out to inspect the tyres and found one to be flat. It had been punctured by a piece of chert flint, the material used by aboriginal peoples to make arrowheads.

This required that I empty the contents of the trunk in order to get the spare wheel. In the two hours this took I became increasingly cold despite the energy I was expending.

One of the items found when unloading the trunk was a half-drunk bottle of whiskey. I did know that it was illegal to travel with open bottles of alcohol on US roads. Thinking back to my close encounter with the Wisconsin Highway Patrol I realised that it would have added to the numerous charges I would no doubt have faced.

The bottle presented me with a quandary. Should it be kept or discarded? Given that it was not my property to dispose of and because I would not be travelling far after entering Alaska I repacked it deep underneath all the other stuff in the trunk.

Travelling north I moved out of the dense boreal forest onto the windswept tundra. The sunless sky created a flat light which merged into the featureless landscape. It became more back-woodsy with tough isolated little communities surprisingly lacking either interest or charm.

The few women in these settlements tended to be heavy-set and masculine. The men gravitated to the town's beer parlour apparently interested only in anaesthetising themselves.

It reminded me of the story about a remote mining town in Australia that wished to attract women. They placed an "editorial advertisement" in a big city newspaper outlining the ten to one ratio between men and women.

A journalist picking up on this story phoned the town

mayor and asked if the opportunities for women were really that good. 'Well,' she said, 'the odds for a woman here are very good, but you have to remember that the goods are also very odd.'

When visible, the sun spent its time low on the horizon. Like a well-meaning but misguided friend it actually made driving more difficult, creating both glare and a slippery film of water on top of the ice. That same sunshine also gave a heavenly pink tinge to the crisp virgin snow covering the frozen lakes surrounded by their motionless fringe of sentry-like spruce trees.

From my moving observatory I saw moose, foxes, caribou, eagles, a lynx, and surprisingly - range horses, which had developed coats as thick as bison.

The owner of one log cabin in which I stayed told me that her husband had come into the house proudly boasting of the wild sheep he had shot in the back yard. He was crest-fallen when he saw that she had just shot a grizzly bear in the front.

She went on to tell me that grizzly bears were very dangerous. Anyone walking in the woods was advised to carry pepper spray and wear little bells on their clothing so that they would not come across a bear unexpectedly. 'Constantly be on the lookout for grizzly bear droppings,' she said. 'You can always recognise those because they have little bells in them.'

That night being still and clear I went outside to look at the stars. To get away from the cabin lights I walked to a clearing about 100 yards away. There seemed to be so many stars: they filled every inch of the sky. Even if the Creator had wanted to, there was no space to squeeze in another even it was a very small one.

Standing in silent awe I was startled, feeling a burst

of wind pressure from their wings as two huge owls flew over me just a couple of feet above my head. I did not hear them at all as these powerful, majestic birds can fly through the woods in complete silence.

Some of the people I met on this journey were almost stereotypical of backwoods types. Dawson Creek has nothing but the Alaska Highway and about four other roads to choose from, yet one local was unable to tell me which one was the Alaska Highway.

It brought to mind a joke another traveller had told me in that town. 'Why could the baby Jesus not have been born in Dawson Creek? Because they couldn't find three wise men and a virgin.'

When I crossed over the Yukon border I was told by a lodge proprietor that most of his guests arrived at about four in the afternoon and left at about 6 A.M. That surprised me because I knew that like me, most people drove all the daylight hours but not during darkness. This would have had them arriving at about 6 P.M. and departing at 8 A.M.

It was only the next morning when I realised I had just crossed a two hour time-zone change but it had not occurred to the lodge owner to mention this detail.

As there was never anywhere else to eat, the lodges provided an evening meal. You ate whatever they had cooked that day. One night we had fish pie made from Arctic char, a poor relation of the salmon. Another evening it was an intensely gamey caribou, stew which though filling it was not particularly to my taste.

While staying in this place a man asked where he could get a haircut. This led to much discussion about locals who fancied their skill with a pair of scissors. In the end he went off to obtain this service from the diesel mechanic.

Driving through an Indian reserve in Montana, I had been disappointed not to see any actual North American Indians. Now in northern Canada, I saw both aboriginal Indians with their lovely thick black hair, and occasionally the more Mongolian looking Inuit peoples. I had learnt to refer to them as Inuit, meaning native-peoples, because the name Eskimo which had been given to them by the white man, simply meant "eater-of-raw-meat" which they considered derogatory.

One place in which I stayed was run by a German couple whose proud boast was that they served the oldest drink in the world. To me it looked like a rather unimaginative rum and Coke.

'But,' said our host 'The secret is the ice chips. They are cut from a nearby glacier. So, by the time it ends up in a drink the ice is thousands of years old.

This same couple appeared to have adopted a Chinese girl, now in her late teens. In this land of predominantly unattractive people her youthful beauty shone like a beacon.

She sat on a bench reading in the room which served as the lodge dining room and sitting area. Her back nestled into the warmth of a decorative, frontier-theme wall-hanging made from luxuriant arctic-fox furs.

Because several other people were there and every movement was so obvious and observed, I foolishly never actually broke ranks and spoke to her. A fellow traveller at my table saw me looking at her, and said: 'Pretty, isn't she? Adopted as a baby from the Ktunaxa First Nations Indian tribe.'

The sleeping accommodation for this lodge consisted of small individual log cabins about the size of a British garden shed. How lucky I was that these were located some distance from the main building, requiring me to go outside.

This allowed me to see the most wonderful sight; the Northern Lights, bewitching green swirls silently making gigantic leaps across the night sky. Sometimes, when less agitated, they simply danced seductively; spiritually other-worldly, mesmerising.

The Vikings thought the strange flashing lights were reflections of the Valkyries' armour as they led Norsemen to their death. Indigenous peoples in Canada thought the lights to be the dancing spirits of children who had died at birth.

Some also thought that a child conceived beneath the Northern lights would be blessed with beauty and wisdom. Perhaps the Ktunaxa girl had been conceived beneath the Northern Lights?

Heating in the cabins was provided by a propane-fuelled potbelly stove. This generated so much sauna-like heat that I turned it down. Exhausted, I fell into bed and was quickly asleep.

In my ensuing dream I was making love to the Ktunaxa girl beneath the Northern lights while lying on a sensual bed of fox furs.

Pleasurable though this reverie was it did not last long. In my attempt to turn down the stove I had inadvertently turned it off and the inside temperature of the cabin plummeted to match the sub-zero outside.

This confirmed I was a cheechako; a newcomer to the north, ignorant of the weather, the animals, the terrain and the culture. The opposite of this was a sourdough, a man with local wisdom, a person physically and emotionally equipped for the rigours of life in this rugged, inhospitable environment.

One bone-fide sourdough I met was Rupert. As he wiped his face with the back of his hand the first thing I noticed were his calloused palms and missing teeth. Stopping quickly to take a pot-shot at a lynx caused a partially filled 50 gallon drum of diesel to break free and roll off the back of his battered pick-up. I helped in the process of decanting the contents into Jerry-cans so that the two of us could lift the drum back onto the truck.

To create a siphon he sucked the diesel through a rubber tube before crimping it off with his thumb and forefinger. Then he spat out the diesel which had reached his mouth with the nonchalance of Californian housewife spitting out Listerine.

'Is this dangerous?' I enquired as diesel splashed all over the place. 'Oh, no,' replied Rupert.

'Under conditions such as we have today you can toss a match into spilt diesel and it will simply go out.' 'NO!' I shouted quickly. 'That's all right: I don't need a demonstration.'

Throughout this process Rupert never stopped talking. In particular he wanted to provide extensive information about the wicked excesses of Anchorage's vice-ridden Fourth Avenue. 'Better still,' he advised, I should join a church. Any church - that way I would be sure to meet a lot of whores.' Rupert, was preoccupied with whores, a word which he pronounced as who-ers.

Driving along after this interlude I saw so much natural beauty. I even wondered if the desperately low temperatures were nature's way of keeping people out of this remote area so that it would remain pristine.

I stopped to take a photograph of a lovely creek, pronounced crik by the locals, with its winding stream frozen solid. Its banks, puffed with globular formations of the whitest snow looked like huge mounds of shaving cream. I just wished I could share this beauty with Dagmar and, strangely for me, I even thought of my family at this time.

Perhaps it was the loneliness.

Approaching the border-crossing* into Alaska there were three cars ahead of me. Observing each one closely I noticed they were processed quickly and waved on. Now at ID-19 it was still completely legal for me to be re-entering the US: I hoped my appearance was one of quiet confidence.

'What's all this stuff in your car?' The officer asked somewhat gruffly.

'What will you be doing in Alaska? 'How long will you be staying?

'Are you registered with the Draft Board?'

That of course was the killer question to which I could legitimately reply yes.

So, it was with mixed feelings that I re-entered the US knowing my timeframe for escape was diminishing.

Arriving in Anchorage the first thing I did was look for a cheap boardinghouse. I slept in a three-man dormitory with a hunter whose enormous belly, silhouetted against the window, rose and fell in time with his thunderous snore. The other man, called Cleveland, would have fitted perfectly in a Robert Service poem of the early 1900s.

Robert Service, who became known as "the Bard

*Footnote

Fortunately this border-crossing was undertaken before computers were in general use. In 1964 and well prior to the Internet, an IBM mainframe computer with less capacity than an early iPhone, occupied an entire room. A room which needed to be cooled to offset the heat generated by its legions of heat producing valves, predecessors of the transistor.

In the same year 1964, Arthur C. Clark, an English science fiction writer (who later co-wrote the screenplay for 'A Space Odyssey') made his audience roar with laughter when he predicted the mobile phone.

of the Yukon," had been born in Lancashire in 1874. Working as a bank clerk in the Yukon he witnessed the harshness and desperation of frontier life and the obsessive behaviour created by the Klondike Gold Rush. Copying the style of his contemporary, Rudyard Kipling, his poems described many of the prospectors and the strange characters he met.

Cleveland's home was an isolated cabin set in the remote bush where he supported himself off the land. He said he could always shoot enough meat to eat, grow vegetables in summertime and sell furs to obtain cash.

He described gathering and eating a delicacy – "chicken of the woods." This orange-sulphur coloured fungus grows 10 inch overlapping plates which emerge from rotting wood in the spring and autumn.

'But you do have to cook it,' he added somewhat unnecessarily. Cook it I thought: I would want to irradiate it.

'There's wood all around me. All I have to do is cut it and it will keep me warm throughout the winter. Anyway, even if I could afford propane it would be useless where I live because it freezes at -40.'

Cleveland mentioned he had four sons; other than that his information was vague. He did not know where two of the sons were and was unsure about the other two. He never mentioned his wife or what had happened to her. Saddest for me was that Cleveland did not really appear to care about anyone.

That evening he asked if I would like to go for a beer, suggesting the Silver Dollar tavern on Fourth Avenue. 'It's well stocked with some real fine who-ers,' he added as inducement.

Setting off for a coffee shop instead, I noticed a deep gaping scar across one road. The still un-mended aftermath of what was referred to as the Great Alaskan earthquake which had occurred on Good Friday 1964. Across South-central Alaska this quake caused ground fissures, collapsing structures and tsunamis, which in total claimed well over 100 lives.

The going rate even in Anchorage for coffee was only ten cents a cup with unlimited refills. Placing my dime on the counter I thought of the coin which had been stuck to my call-up papers: a whole lot of turbulence, effort and emotional sadness with the only net gain - a dime.

Asking to use the phone, it was immediately placed on the counter. Calling the owners of the car I was delivering, they suggested we should meet in the Cheechako bar at 10 o'clock next morning.

The Konigs, who both worked for the railway company, had been in the bar for about 20 minutes by the time I arrived. Mrs. Konig had already enjoyed her first rum and coke of the day and her husband had almost finished his beer.

They were told about the puncture and the stone chip on the windscreen. Neither seemed to worry them; these being par for the course for anyone driving up the Alaska Highway.

They paid me the balance of the money due without quibbling. I had to force them to leave their warm perches and go out to inspect the vehicle. Back in the bar, the Konigs needed to complete some paperwork, commenting on the condition of the car and their satisfaction with the driver.

Mr. Konig started to write across the form, 'I would trust this man with a...' before turning to me and asking, 'How do you spell Rolls-Royce?'

As I left the bar they were ordering another round. I knew Mr. Konig was then going to the rail depot where, alarmingly, his work involved signalling. I also wondered how Mrs. Konig would manage to drive home, especially as the black ice on Anchorage's streets made a mockery of stop signs and traffic lights.

It had been my intention to buy a passage on a freighter travelling between Anchorage and Tokyo which I considered to be a stepping stone en-route to south-east Asia and eventually India. Unable to find a suitable ship and already down to a minimally safe ID-18, I had no choice but to buy an expensive airline ticket.

The 24 hour wait before my flight departure gave me a lot of time to reflect. My thoughts were primarily of Dagmar. She had given me so much and was so important in my life. She had taught me to have fun and to be uninhibitedly playful. She had shown me that sex did not have to be taken seriously. It could be light-hearted as well as romantic and passionate.

When any of us travel we are force-fed so many new experiences. Short periods of time become the stimuli-saturated equivalent of elongated periods of normality.

I felt Dagmar was both very close and also very distant. We had been in each other's arms a little over two weeks ago. Now 4700 miles and numerous un-shared experiences apart. More significant and symbolic was that I would shortly be leaving North America. Moving away from - not towards her.

The plane doors closed, but there appeared to be some delay before departure. Anyone with a guilty conscience worries unnecessarily, but on this occasion the delay was merely routine. A tanker truck drew up beside the plane and using a high pressure jet, de-iced the wings.

When the plane started to taxi along the runway I allowed myself a gasp of relief. So many things had been weighing on my mind. Imminently I would be out of the clutches of American officialdom and both the army and jail would no longer be a possibility.

As important as my personal needs, had been the feeling that if I got into serious trouble it would cause my parents so much distress. It would have been an agonising burden for them.

The man sitting beside me on the plane who smoked one cigarette after another, became increasingly annoyed with the passenger in front of him. On a couple of occasions she pushed her bag so far back it ended up at his feet.

On the third occasion he noticed a bottle of duty-free whiskey peering out of this bag. Retrieving the bottle he broke the seal and silently withdrew the cork, took a mouthful and offered it to me. We each had another swig before he returned the bottle to the bag, zipped it up and pushed it forwards.

As the plane travelled through the night sky I studied the school atlas and distractedly thought of myself as the pen nib tracing a thin line on a global barograph.

Chapter 9

JAPAN

Arriving in Japan completely unprepared and with nowhere to stay, I boarded an airport bus heading into Tokyo. The driver wanted to know where he should drop me off, but all I could say was 'ryokan' - the word for a traditional Japanese inn.

The driver proved to be extremely kind and went to great lengths, eventually finding a ryokan in which I could stay for two days. I tried to give him a tip which was graciously declined, causing me to feel embarrassed at having made my first social blunder in Japan. I did not wish to offend the courteous and supportive driver who had done so much for me.

Every experience I had of Japanese people on that visit showed them to be well-mannered, gentle and charming. Yet, this was a mere fifteen years after Mr Jones' terrible ordeal on the Burma railway. Maybe all human beings retain some genes from Hecate, the Greek goddess capable of both good and evil.

I removed my shoes in the vestibule of the ryokan before putting on slippers, which were themselves to be removed before entering my room. The paper-thin fusuma doors slid apart revealing a sparsely furnished room.

On the floor were tatami mats, a low kotatsu table, a few floor cushions and a thin sleeping futon, which was obviously too short for me. The innkeeper smiled as he peered up at me, and said in broken English: 'Mr. King very high,' before shuffling off to find additional bedding.

As instructed I changed into the yukata, the informal kimono traditionally worn by both men and women. This simple act instantly transformed me - I now felt different. This above-all symbolised I was in an entirely different culture. I had been required to, or was it "invited" to relinquish the most obvious symbol of Western culture.

After a bowl of green tea I was taken to see the washing arrangements. The squat design of the lavatories did not concern me, but the fact that they were used by both genders of all ages, and were open to public view, did catch me by surprise.

In my home, bodily functions were rarely mentioned. If they were it was in hushed tones with a sense of embarrassment that human bodies could be so animalistic and disgusting. I never heard my parents use the word "buttocks", only euphemisms such as bottom which was to them, clearly, an unclean part of the body.

As far as bathing was concerned I soon learned that the deep, narrow tub filled with hot water was not to be used for washing; this was purely for relaxation after I had washed.

It also became apparent there was a large staff of young girls who meticulously cleaned every inch of the establishment. They seemed to be ever-present, regardless of whether I was bathing, brushing my teeth in the fifteen-foot long communal wooden trough, or doing anything else.

Despite the lack of privacy everyone was friendly, courteous and respectful. Everyone bowed deeply to me on every possible occasion. This was a major contrast to the rectory in which I had always been taught humility to the point of subservience. Now it was impossible not to feel elevated, yet at the same time my fragile self-esteem made me feel like an imposter, unworthy of the exalted treatment I was receiving.

There is only one place in Tokyo's Chioda district from which you can glimpse a small corner of the Imperial Palace, then home of Emperor Hirohito and Empress Nagako.

Distractedly looking across the moat up to the highly traditional Zen-style building, I noticed a few people surreptitiously coming close to me in order to have their photograph taken. For the Japanese at this important location, I, at six foot two with fair colouring seemed to be as interesting as the palace itself.

I wandered around many back streets with their noodle stalls, conscious of the ever present smell of fish: becoming aware of how physically small the people were and the elegance of women in their kimonos. Everyone worked so tirelessly; I felt sure Japan would rise to prominence after its still comparatively recent nuclear devastation.

On my third day in Tokyo, when I was due to leave the ryokan, something remarkable and fortuitous happened. Walking along the street I saw Tucker Smith, one of the dancers from the New York pavilion. He had dyed his hair a weird custard-yellow and was signing autographs for the mob of young girls surrounding him.

Unbeknown to me, West Side Story was playing in Tokyo and Tucker, who had been one of the Jets in the film was part of the cast. It would be hard to tell who was more surprised and shocked at seeing each other. He was not particularly warm or friendly, especially as the Japanese girls, assuming I was part of the West Side Story cast, crowded round me asking for my autograph instead of his. But hey! I didn't expect ever to receive rock-star treatment again and so was happy to sign a few of their programs.

Paradoxically this may have given the girls wanting autographs as much pleasure as they would have received from a bone fide cast member. As in the art world, if you believe a fake to be real it can give you as much satisfaction as the genuine article.

A few feet further on, Ben Gerard, another former pavilion actor and cast member of West Side Story was also signing autographs. In contrast, Ben proved to be incredibly warm and supportive, to the point of taking me back to the modern Western-style hotel in which they were all staying and arranging for me to get the same discounted room rate. Later, he also took me to the Nissei theatre and showed me his dressing room.

Despite the advantageous room-rate I found everything to be so expensive in Japan that I decided to confirm my onward travel to Hong Kong. By coincidence, my last evening in Tokyo was also the last evening at which the West Side Story cast would be there.

Entering the hotel lobby at about 6 p.m. on that day there was a buzz of activity. Although this had nothing to do with me, I once again sensed the excitement of a theatre group being together. Heading for the elevator, Ben saw me, and said that there was a drinks party due to start shortly in the eighth floor suite they had used as a briefing room.

'Come along if you would like to,' he said. 'It's our last night in Tokyo. We leave first thing in the morning for Osaka.' After shaving and showering I went to the eighth floor where there was already much activity.

Although I had been invited I felt like an interloper and stayed at the back of the room just to observe.

Everyone was in high spirits, both literally and metaphorically. There were so many bottles of whiskey I thought the Suntory distillery must have sponsored the gathering. The conversations overheard revolved around which restaurant they were going to that night and the clubs they would visit later.

For the duration of their time in Tokyo the group had been accompanied by a translator-cum-organizer. I had noticed her a couple of times, always dressed traditionally in a kimono as she made arrangements with hotel staff and drivers. That night she looked different, still very Japanese but wearing a burgundy, floor-length wrap-around dress with a Nehru collar.

The cast generously proposed a toast of gratitude to her: jokingly adding they had nicknamed her the Mikado because they had to obey all her commands. She smiled as for a brief moment as the spotlight swung from the actors and onto her.

A little later she came up to me, introducing herself saying. 'Don't believe that nonsense about me being the Mikado. I have not had any heads chopped off yet - but it could still happen; some of them are very naughty,' she said with a laugh.

'My name is Mitsuko. I have seen you talking to some of the cast members but as you are not a part of their group - what are you doing here?' I told her about having been in New York and the coincidence of being in Tokyo at the same time as the West Side Story production, but that I too would be leaving tomorrow.

As the room started to empty she wandered off and chatted with a couple of other people before returning to me, and saying. 'There is a lot of food here and this will be my dinner. If you'd like to join me we could eat together.' A free meal and someone to talk to sounded irresistible. 'Come back in an hour,' she said.

When I returned, the suite had been cleaned and tidied but there was still an odour of whiskey and food. For that reason she had the staff lay up a small table in her room which connected to the meeting area.

As this was a modern western-style hotel it had a sound-system similar to one in the American chemical company's hotel. A switch on the bedside table gave access to four music channels. Mitsuko had selected the Japanese genre from which came the slightly rasping, husky tones of a shakuhachi bamboo flute playing a slow, calming piece.

Mitsuko's movements were all deliberate and unhurried; everything she did was undertaken with thought and care. She smiled and I felt instantly at ease as she ushered me to sit down. Although there had been a lot of food at the reception I had not noticed the small dishes of sushi which were now on the table. Nor had I seen the small earthenware flagon of sake resting in a warming bowl.

As I fumbled with my chopsticks she knelt beside me in a way you would only ever experience in the Orient. Taking my right hand first and then my left, she carefully examined them, commenting on how long my fingers were and what graceful hands I had. Then guiding me to use the chopsticks she showed me the first of many things I would learn from her that night.

She asked my age and was momentarily startled when I said 21. Quick-wittedly she smiled and said. 'That gives us an average age of 30, which is a perfect balance - a good omen.'

She asked if I had a girlfriend and I poured out my

heart about Dagmar. I told her how much I loved her, how much fun we had together and how terribly I was missing her. More for my benefit than hers, I enthused at length about going to parties and dancing together.

'What do you think your future will be together?' she gently enquired. Guessing from my demeanour and the pause before an incoherent reply, it was a painful question for which I had no firm answer.

After a brief silence and when prompted by a question from me, she spoke of having been married for fifteen years.

'Like three quarters of all marriages in Japan, it had been arranged by my parents,' she said. 'My husband is a good man, what we call a "salary man." He works long hours for Hitachi Electronics Corporation and then does what is expected of him and every other businessman. He goes with his colleagues to the Shinjuku entertainment district before stumbling home late most evenings.'

She was not critical of her husband or disparaging about her marriage. This is just the way it was. The lives of all the women she grew up with were the same, she said. Many of them had been blessed with children – but not her.

She went on to tell me about her work. After studying English she had increasingly been asked to act as a translator. Sometimes working with diplomatic missions, occasionally with businessmen, but her preference was anything related to the arts.

This was the first time she had assisted with an American theatrical group. It was fun she said, but they are like unruly children; difficult to organise.

Changing the topic she asked if I had enjoyed my brief time in Tokyo and if I had seen and experienced everything I wanted to.

'My time in the ryokan was a wonderful experience,' I said. 'It was so special for me to change into the yakuta and become transformed by the simplicity of my surroundings and the kindness of my host.'

It pleased her that I enjoyed and appreciated Japanese tradition. 'Is there anything else you would like to have seen or done during your visit? She enquired.

'Well,' I said, 'I have heard a lot about the ancient city of Kyoto and am sorry not to have had sufficient funds to spend time there. I have also heard about the special Japanese bathing ceremonies and would like to have experienced one of those.'

'Oh,' she said 'you mean ofuro the honourable purification bath which people undertake when visiting a temple?' 'Yes, that's it,' I muttered.

'Well, I cannot take you to Kyoto and there is no time for you to do ofuro. But under this auspicious full moon I can give you a special Japanese cleansing bath,' she said with an enigmatic smile.

I heard the bathwater running for sometime before she re-emerged. Gliding out of the bathroom which was now lit with catering candles, she sat on my lap with the confidence of a long-term lover. After kissing me lightly on the lips she gently stroked my face and slowly ran her fingers through my hair.

It was obvious she was studying my face as she commented on the shape of my eyes and their greenish-blue colour.

Following her lead I reciprocated by gently kissing her on the forehead and cheeks before moving my lips to hers.

Standing up she slowly unbuttoned my shirt. Rising

up on tiptoe she kissed my neck and chest; then as the cuffs were loosened she kissed my wrists.

She indicated her wrap-around velvet dress was fastened with small press studs which separated easily. When both naked she led me into the bathroom and bade me kneel in the tub. Using a small sea-sponge scented with sandalwood oil from the bath, she cleansed me slowly and meticulously. Starting with my head she washed my forehead, ears and neck. Maintaining the same attention to detail she worked down both the back and front of my body.

As she stepped into the bath and knelt in front of me it was obvious that it was now my turn to bathe her. So I too meticulously washed her petite body, all the while alternating my gaze between the area I was washing and her eyes. In turn I too lingered to appreciate the beauty of her lovely almond-shaped eyes.

We towel-dried each other but because of the height difference she had me kneel and then proceeded playfully to dry my hair. Her own hair which had been tied in a bun was now released and fell to her shoulders.

Lying on my back she slowly butterfly-kissed and nibbled her way from head to toe, occasionally making little sniffing noises. Apart from letting her breasts brush my penis that poor chap had received little attention until her tongue started to trace patterns along my inner thighs. After what seemed like an agonisingly prolonged wait, I was rewarded with pleasure and relief.

Both satisfied with the outcome we sat up in the bed and celebrated by sipping two small mugs of warm sake.

'Now,' she said, 'it is for you to give to me, all that I have I given to you.' Thus began my guidance and real initiation in how to please a woman.

The first thing I had learned was to slow down and savour every moment. To be guilt-free and relish all the pleasures the five senses could deliver.

As Mitsuko guided and encouraged me we made love another three or four times. On each occasion she introduced variation, something that for me, was new and exhilarating.

Curling into a foetal ball she enveloped herself in my arms. We rested for an hour or two before she finally said, 'You know I have to be in the lobby by eight o'clock to round up the children. It is now time for you to return your room.'

Even this dismissal was done gently and with style. I told Mitsuko how exquisitely beautiful and feminine she was and I thanked her for the loving gift she had bestowed on me.

She surprised me by saying:

'It is I who must thank you. You have shared your youth, your beauty and your energy with me. You have given me the most precious gift possible: the feeling of being young and desired.'

Having staggered back to my room I lay dazed on the bed. I was euphoric, invincible, transformed. Forever changed. Deliriously high on the most exhilarating drug - dopamine.

Chapter 10

HONG KONG

In the morning I went to the hotel lobby a few minutes before 9 A.M. and stood quietly to one side of the entrance door. Mitsuko was rounding up the last stragglers, directing them to the coaches. She circled the room saying farewell to the hotel staff, bowing ceremonially to each of them.

Standing in front of me she paused fractionally longer than she had with others. She bowed gracefully and with her back to the room, it was only I who had the privilege to enjoy her beaming smile.

On my arrival in Hong Kong, I once again had to get into the centre of town and find a place to stay. Hong Kong was easier in that it was English-speaking and had the required form of cheap accommodation, a YMCA.

Actually it had two YMCA's, one of which was designated as being for Chinese. Choosing the other, on the basis of language rather than race, I set about negotiating the bus routes to Kowloon.

After checking in I lugged my suitcase up three flights of stairs. Entering the room I was startled to find there was already someone there, a rough looking Chinese man of about 30. It wasn't that I minded sharing it was just that in my fatigued and fragile state I was irritable and merely wanted to collapse onto the bed.

The Chinese chap, to whom I had not been particularly courteous, sensitively said he would go out and leave me to use the facilities and rest. After showering I simply wrapped a towel around my waist and fell onto the vacant bed.

Despite being totally exhausted, sleep did not come. The hot, airless room was partly to blame but the real problem was that in an almost delirious way, I kept re-winding the events of the past 24 hours.

In particular, valuing Mitsuko's comment that she would retain the memory of our night together as if it was encased in a droplet of amber.

Feeling better in the morning, I was looking forward to exploring Hong Kong. It turned out that my roommate was a doctor. Somehow that made me feel better and I regretted having been suspicious of someone who had displayed nothing but courtesy and openness. He even suggested places I might like to visit.

Hong Kong was everything I expected. Most of the poorer women were wearing samfoo, a waisted blouse with toggle closures and baggy, lower-calf length trousers. In one of the parks a group of elderly men and women were practising tai chi. They moved with a spiritual grace which belied the difficulty of the postures they held.

More affluent women were delightfully feminine and elegant. Younger women looked incredibly sexy in their cheongsams, the thigh-revealing, slit-up-the-side skirts which reminded me of the film, The World of Susie Wong.

So enamoured was I with cheongsams that I bought one and sent it to Dagmar. I thought she would look as amazing and sexy as all of these Chinese girls. It was only months later that I realised the foolishness of what

I had done.

First of all what I had bought was clearly designed for the tourist market. It was a garishly bright red and there would be absolutely no occasion on which Dagmar would wear it other than to a fancy dress party.

Equally ridiculous was the fact that I knew nothing about dress sizes and the shop merely assumed my Caucasian girlfriend would be substantially larger than a Chinese woman.

Alternatively, it could have been that when I said she was 22 the shopkeeper thought I was referring to dress size rather than her age. The result was money wasted buying an oversized, unwanted garment solely to indulge my fantasies.

The British in Hong Kong were ultra-traditional, wearing double-breasted, brass-buttoned blazers, regimental ties and Panama hats. They could have been swept up from the Members' Enclosure at Lord's Cricket ground and deposited in this colonial outpost, unaware that their playground lay in the shadow of an enormous and increasingly hostile China.

Taking the Star Ferry from Kowloon across to Hong Kong Island I made my way to the port of Aberdeen. This was one of the most sensational sights I could have imagined. A hive of activity with bumboats plying their trade and hundreds of sampans, cross-paddled from the rear by coolie-hatted women. Whole families living every aspect of their lives on what the Chinese called 'jung' or floating homes.

The British, never careful with the pronunciation of foreign languages, referred to these flat-bottomed, lug-rigged seagoing houses as Junks. If anything captured the essence of the orient it was this harbour. I was mesmerised by the exotic scene: this was what I had travelled to the other side of the world to see.

There was an unforgiving sense of hardness to Hong Kong. The courtesy I had enjoyed in Japan during the preceding days had come to an abrupt halt and the requirement to tip on every occasion was obvious.

An absolutely charming tailor plied me with strong beer and brought out ever increasingly expensive bales of cloth. I had intended to purchase an inexpensive lightweight suit which I considered to be a modest investment and was happy to proceed with this man.

A day or two later when I was passing the same shop, the tailor was offhand and rude. He knew he had extracted all the money he was going to prise out of me and now clearly saw no further need for civility let alone the provision of beer.

On the return ferry from Wanchai across Victoria harbour to Kowloon I met Dr. Fenton, a middle-aged Englishman who told me a sad and horrific story. His wife had been murdered in India by a gang of thieves who stabbed her mercilessly and totally unnecessarily.

Apart from the obvious misery of the story it alerted me to the reality that submerged below the exoticism was the potential for real danger. I had grown up in an environment where violence was almost unknown. Now I was dangerously over-confident of my personal safety in these different cultures.

Returning to the YMCA I thought it was time to sort out the jumble of clothes in my ancient 'expander' suitcase. Moving most of my crumpled clothes onto the bed I decided to keep only the necessary minimum for my onward travel. Ahead of me lay exploration of South East Asia before returning to England overland from India.

I departed Hong Kong's Kai Tak airport at night.

As was normal in those days, the plane had only two classes, standard and first-class. Despite my basic ticket I learned on boarding, a first-class seat had been allocated to me. Was this a purely a logistical matter or had my youthful enthusiasm and courtesy prompted some type of altruism with the check-in staff?

As an inexperienced traveller I always chose a window seat and on this occasion, it proved to be the right decision. The aerial view of the Hong Kong waterfront reflecting its myriad coloured lights was sensational.

The enormous, gaudily-lit floating restaurants in Aberdeen harbour juxtaposed with the unlit, eerily sinister junks. A scene like that depicted in a child's fairy-story; an over-simplification of that which is clearly seen and understood and that which is veiled and mysterious.

Light and darkness in their traditional roles, representing what is welcoming and that which is ominous. A magical vision for me in my first class seat which was soon to be followed by champagne and delicious food.

Life - I thought, really was rather wonderful.

Chapter 11

THAILAND

Travelling into Bangkok on the bus from Don Muang airport I got into conversation with a youngish American called Gary. As both of us were travelling on our own, we decided to find a hotel together and share a room. Gary had been told about a place called the Trocadero and that is where we went.

He indicated that despite being inexpensive, the Trocadero was one of the oldest and best hotels in Bangkok. On arrival I could fully believe it was one of the oldest but if it had ever been one of the best, it certainly did not deserve that accolade now.

Everything in the hotel was threadbare and worn. At breakfast there was an attempt to display old-world style by using silver-plated cutlery, the effect being somewhat negated by the heavy tarnish and green encrustation found between the prongs of the forks. Despite this I had my first taste of papaya which I thought delicious.

Endeavouring to emulate European-style service there was a sign on the bedside table in English which read, 'You are invited to take advantage of the chambermaid.'

Still laughing at this we departed for the Jim Thompson silk emporium. Sadly, we did not meet Mr. Thompson himself. At that time he was probably the most famous Westerner in Southeast Asia, having been credited with saving the Thai silk industry.

The usually quiet Gary surprised me by coming out with a joke. 'Did you hear about the two silkworms having a race,' he said. 'They ended in a tie.'

That evening, sitting in a restaurant where many of the patrons were speaking English, an overweight Indian man walked in and sat down. Despite the restaurant being obviously busy he repeatedly snapped his fingers at the harried waitress.

Finally losing patience, she shouted at him across the crowded restaurant, 'It takes more than two fingers to make me come.'

We set out to find the floating market which we understood to be in the centre of Bangkok but turned out to be some distance away. Completely lost we were eventually stopped by a Buddhist monk, called Prayed, who wanted to practice his English.

In this man we were to acquire a wonderful guide who took us everywhere in Bangkok, from the temple of the Emerald Buddha to the tributaries of the mighty Chao Praya river.

As a monk, the portly Prayed only had to stand by the side of the road and look towards any vacant taxi or songthaew (a two-bench truck vehicle) and it would immediately stop for him. Gary and I later joked that Prayed was enjoying travelling all over Bangkok by taxi at our expense. But it was certainly worth it as we saw so many interesting places and met many people we would not have done it any other way.

Two days later when Gary left to take up a job in Seoul, I gratefully accepted Prayed's offer to move into a room in his monastery. Each day I learned more about Prayed and monastic life - a life of ordained humility.

At five A.M. the huge drum mounted high in the

centre of the temple complex was sounded, gently at first and then with increasing vigour. By one minute past five it was not possible for anyone, including me, to remain asleep.

The monks filed sleepily into their first meditation session of the day prior to collecting their begging bowls and heading out onto the streets. They were only allowed eight possessions, one of which was the begging bowl. The remaining seven included their three-piece saffron robe, a girdle, water bottle and filter, a needle to repair their robe, and a razor to shave their head.

When the head is first ceremonially shaved it is indicative of moving into a new life, a form of cleansing similar to baptism. As an ongoing practice it is a renunciation of physical beauty and personal vanity.

Prayed, whose late father had been a clerk in the civil service, came from a middle-class, literate family. He said that all young men from every background were expected at some time to spend two years studying as a Buddhist monk while living in a monastery. This accorded him and his entire family a huge amount of respect.

He went on to say, 'Being a monk allows me to contemplate the relevance of spirituality, to temporarily step aside from ambition and physical desire.' Then with a broad smile he added, 'but I am looking forward to being in bed with a woman again.'

My favourite time in the monastery was five P.M. when the monks filed into the central temple hall with its array of gilded Buddha statues. Sometimes I would sit unobtrusively just inside the door, becoming lost in their hypnotic chanting.

Prayed was the only monk in the temple who spoke

any English. In an area restricted to men only, he proudly showed me a sign he had painted which read, 'Do not enter a woman.'

He took me to meet some of his relatives. When a drink of water was served by his mother it had to be given to me first and then passed to Prayed. As a monk, he could not be alone in a room with a woman and could not receive anything directly from a woman, even if she was a close relative.

With Prayed I eventually got to see the fabled floating market. For a mere two dollars I rented a huge boat with its noisy, one-lung single-cylinder diesel motor and long-tail propeller. The whole boat shook so relentlessly I thought my automatic watch, a fake Rolex purchased in Hong Kong, would remain fully wound for a month.

We went through rivers and canals whose banks were covered with dense jungle vegetation and palm trees. The waterlogged teak timbers of the wooden shacks sagging into the muddy water - the same water in which people washed and from which they filled their cooking pots and drinking vessels.

Prayed directed the boat until we stopped at a small, unimposing waterside temple. What he wanted to show me was a large spreading tree draped in a saffron girdle which signified that it had been ordained as an honorary monk, and as such was protected.

'These special Rain Trees,' he said, 'fold their leaves inwards during rain which in turn allows the rain to fall through to the ground and then reach the roots.

'Notice how lush the grass is under the tree; this is not only due to the rain but because cicadas feeding on the leaves drop a honeydew-like secretion which falls to enrich the soil.' He said no more but the smile on his face indicated the pleasure he took from the wonders of nature.

The floating market was remarkable; jam- packed with small boats all heavily-laden with fruit and vegetables. Each skiff was skilfully manoeuvred in the crowded waterway by a peasant woman wearing a traditional, lampshade sun-hat. It was a working local scene of no interest to the American serviceman on R&R in Bangkok and as yet undiscovered by the limited number of bona fide tourists.

One place in the world I really wanted to see it was the vast temple complex at Angkor in Cambodia. As a schoolboy I had seen an article in National Geographic magazine showing the magnificent "lost" temples which had been overgrown and consumed by the jungle. Massive vines with the girth of a tree having shifted and split apart the gigantic blocks of stone had left an eerie, disconcerting scene.

If I could have changed places with anyone from history it would have been the French naturalist and explorer, Henri Mouhot. He is still credited with hacking his way through the jungle and discovering this "lost civilisation." A real-life Rider Haggard adventure.

Having succeeded in getting a Cambodian visa I was unable to obtain a re-entry permit for Thailand. As my only way out of Cambodia would have been into war-torn Vietnam, this was clearly not a good idea. The Vietcong would probably not ask to see my passport before shooting and the last thing I wished to do was seek assistance from the American military.

But I made a promise to myself that one day I, too, like Henri Mouhot would gaze in awe at the remote temples of Angkor. Prayed's advice was that I should visit a similar Khmer temple located at Phimae. I travelled all day on three filthy, overcrowded buses bedecked with Buddhist pictures and floral arrangements. On arrival I felt deflated and disappointed, finding only one relatively small temple. Saddest of all was that because I felt disappointed I did not even appreciate the single Khmer-style temple that was there.

Wandering around at dusk I was approached by two young students who lived on the outskirts of the village. When they understood that I had nowhere to stay that night, they invited me back to their home. This consisted of small wooden structure with a high, steeply-pitched Thai-style roof designed to let the hot air escape. It was built on stilts to keep it above flood waters and had steep steps rising to the entrance door.

It was hard for me to work out the family relationships. There were two young children who were petrified of me, never before having encountered tall, fair-haired giants and there was an old woman whom I thought more likely to be the grandmother of the boys than their mother.

The single room was dominated by a large bed enclosed in a mosquito net. Shortly after dark and despite my protestations that I was happy to sleep on the floor, the grandmother insisted I should get onto the large bed. The two students climbed in on either side of me.

It felt bad to be usurping the grandmother's bed. Having two strange boys sleeping on either side of me was also peculiar. But the boys appeared relaxed, as if this was quite normal to them. We all yielded to sleep, until being woken at first light by the sounds of a pig rooting around close to the hut.

I was not sure where the grandmother had slept that night but thought it was probably on the floor. With a more positive outlook I revisited the temple which was being excavated by numerous young women. I was told they only earned a mere 50 cents for undertaking heavy labour throughout the intense heat of the day.

Then I travelled on to visit a leper colony in Khon Kaen, to which I had been invited by the American missionary who managed it. On arrival the missionary recognised me and was well aware of our casual encounter in Bangkok, but made no effort to welcome me in any way: not even offering the customary glass of water.

An interesting contrast between the open generosity of a local Thai family and a bland, self-righteous Westerner reneging on what had presumably been an insincere invitation.

Another reminder of the widely held opinion that the strange denizens of backwaters such as this came from the ranks of mercenaries, misfits and (mendacious) missionaries.

Late that night en route to Bangkok, the bus in which I was travelling broke down just outside the town of Prachin Buri. A tuk-tuk driver approached me asking if I wanted a place to stay. I indicated that I did, stressing that it must be close and inexpensive.

Instead of staying close by the tuk tuk seemed to go further and further out of town. The place to which I was taken was more like a bar, in which there were a few local men and several bored-looking women.

No one spoke any English and getting a room seemed to be impossible. After much haggling it became obvious that the only way to get a room was to choose a woman first. I chose one at random and we went upstairs to a bedroom where my first priority was to have a shower. She then showered before getting into bed beside me.

The bed was very narrow; if they considered this to

be suitable for two people it must have been because they anticipated the occupants would be stacked. The young woman was totally perplexed as to why I had come to a brothel, chosen a 'girl' and then only wanted to sleep.

There are some situations you cannot easily explain with sign language and this was one of them. The girl looked dejected, indicating she thought I did not find her attractive. While this was true I did my best to give her face-saving assurance that she was in no way to blame. It was I who was tired and "not up to it."

In the morning the tuk tuk driver was waiting with a broad, toothless grin. He had spent the whole night waiting, but for him this was a good deal. Not only was he paid by me but no doubt received a kickback from the "hotel."

Prayed informed me that there would be a full moon that night. Moreover, as it was the twelfth month in the Thai lunar calendar, it was the day of the special Buddhist festival, Loy Krathong.

Many people would decorate their houses, gardens and temples with intricately shaped paper lanterns. Some, lit with a candle, would be carried dangling beneath a stick. Others were so intricately cut they revolved due to the heat generated by their candle. Loy or loi, literally means to float, and krathong referred to a lotus-shaped receptacle made from either banana leaves or tree bark.

We went to an area in which a small river had broadened out into something like a large pond. It had the advantage of a walkway between the houses and the water. This path was now crowded with cheerful, multigenerational families all eagerly launching their candlelit krathongs.

As the krathongs float away they symbolise the letting go of past transgressions and any ill feelings. Merit is important in both Thailand and Buddhist culture. The krathongs were an offering of gratitude to the Water Goddess and also a vehicle of purification. Burning joss sticks infused the air with aromatic incense and once again I felt exhilarated: so lucky to be a part of this exotic scene.

Having said that, it was now time to move on. In the process of bidding farewell to Prayed, I was surprised and offended to be asked for money; after all, he had invited me to stay in the monastery. Grudgingly, I handed over a few ungenerous baht and departed in a childishly bad mood.

Using a mixture of low denomination Thai baht and American dollars I purchased a third-class ticket to Hat Yai at the extreme southern tip of Thailand. I was genuinely sorry to be leaving Bangkok, the city in which I had watched Muay Thai boxing, experienced the festival of Loy Krathong and laughed with a Buddhist monk while chugging down backwaters of the Chao Phraya river.

Chapter 12

MALAYA

Amid clouds of hissing steam and with much effort the ancient locomotive dragged itself out of Bangkok's urban sprawl. Settling into a slow repetitive rhythm the train chugged into the jungle-covered isthmus leading to the Malay border.

The ambling speed allowed abundant opportunities to study the small kampongs and villages along the route. Frequent stops provided the chance to purchase food, mostly bunches of indigenous little finger bananas.

Given my height and colouring I did stand out, but this attention was shared with a tall, fair-haired young German called Klaus Bettenhausen. The two of us caught each other's eye and burst out laughing when a man who looked like a four-star general moved through the train. His brass-buttoned, khaki uniform had magnificent gold epaulettes and he exuded a confident air of command. His grandeur far exceeding his function of ticket inspector.

Klaus said, 'When I was in India I always tried to travel on the roof of the train. It's so much fun.' Just as I was about to suggest we go up onto the roof of this train he added, 'Unfortunately we cannot do that here in Thailand. Not only are the authorities stricter but there are often water pipes or other things overhead which could prove lethal.'

We hitch-hiked from Hat Yai to Kuala Lumpur. To say we hitch-hiked the whole way is not strictly accurate. At the border crossing into Malaya, I approached a smartly dressed Chinese man who was travelling alone in a large black Mercedes. The businessman reluctantly agreed to give us a ride and opened an immaculately clean boot into which we deposited our dusty backpacks.

Klaus was a seasoned and experienced traveller. On one occasion following a trishaw ride he noticed the vehicle lacked its traditional sunshade. As he had an old parasol acquired in Cambodia he came to an arrangement whereby the latter was taken as payment for the ride.

We took many more trishaw rides together and must have looked very odd: two tall, gangly, pale-skinned men squashed together and constantly laughing for no apparent reason.

'Saw a sign yesterday,' said Klaus, 'It read Hot Bowel of Soup.'

'That must have been in the Thai Tanic restaurant,' I retorted.

Not to be outdone he carried on.

'Met a girl in a bar whose name was Lee Ki Su. Didn't fancy her.'

'Talking about funny signs,' Klaus continued... 'The one I liked most, read Pho King Good. 'Better than Phuc U To.'

Staying in the Kuala Lumpur YMCA was a remarkable man for whom I developed both affection and respect. Lionel Fuller was 82 years old and had lived most of his working life in India as a Colonial Forestry Officer.

Becoming bored with retirement in a tiny cottage

in his native Ireland and despite the limitations of a meagre pension he set out alone, to travel. How different to all those geriatrics found in coastal town rest homes who give in to the assumption that decline comes automatically with age.

Lionel dressed in baggy khaki shorts and a matching short-sleeved shirt. Together with knee-high, olive-green woollen socks he wore a pair of well-used but sturdy brogue shoes which he polished meticulously every evening. His broad-brimmed hat typified the practical headgear of Europeans who had worked outdoors in the tropics.

Lionel, who must have been born in about 1881, was therefore approximately the same age as my much loved old Grandmother. He told me about his early days as a trainee forester in turn-of-the-century East Africa.

'You know, all the women were bare-breasted. It shocked me at first but I soon became used to it, and like everyone else, thought nothing of it.' Then, looking down he said, 'Well, with the exception of one girl. She was the cook's daughter. We exchanged glances but there was never more to it than that.'

I sensed his long-remembered glow of affection, and the regret of unfulfilled desire. It struck me that all of us retain memories of those things which have been significant, perhaps even painful to us. Lionel's search for knowledge, adventure and sex was not dissimilar to my own. It had just occurred 60 years earlier.

Lionel talked of the various countries in which he had worked. Understandably for someone of his age and background it was not surprising he lamented the loss of so many former British colonies. 'It's not just places like the Gold Coast and Nigeria,' he said. 'Rhodesia will be receiving independence later this year.'

After pausing for thought he smiled and said, 'You know the British and French always had different priorities and dissimilar styles of colonial rule. The British left efficient postal systems, far-reaching rail networks and a functioning civil service. The French on the other hand left Indochina with a legacy reflecting their priorities. The three "B"s. Bars, boulevards and brothels.'

Lionel must have taken pleasure from the now rare privilege of being noticed and heard, receiving from me a level of respect few others were sensitive enough or wise enough to accord him. Lionel reminded me of an elderly gentleman whom my father had asked me to visit in Seavale.

Lt-Colonel Westmacott was bedridden and apart from his former nurse who was now his wife, was in contact with no one. Reluctantly, I started making visits to the tiny house in which he lived.

The aptly named Pebble Cottage had been built in the 1700s from stones brought up from the seashore by fishermen. It was sharply triangular in shape, sitting like a wedge in the middle of the road leading out of the village, causing traffic to pass noisily on either side.

As a boy in my early teens I was unimpressed by the sight of a virtually immobile old man with traces of saliva escaping from one side of his mouth. I found it incredible to think that this man, who had been injured during the First World War, had endured ongoing decline for over 40 years.

Seeing him in such a reduced state belied the optimistic and privileged start to his life. After Eton College and Sandhurst he was commissioned before going to South Africa to fight in the second Boer war. He had been much the same age as, and in the same places as Winston Churchill during those years.

After I had been visiting Col. Westmacott regularly for a couple of years, the old man gave me a gift which was precious to us both. It was a Mauser rifle, which the young subaltern, while serving under Colonel Baden-Powell, had acquired from the enemy following the relief of Mafeking. I never knew the exact details but when cleaning the rifle I often wondered about its history. Had this particular rifle ever shot a British soldier? Had the old colonel killed its Boer owner?

Whatever the facts, when I held that rifle I was aware of my direct link with a battlefield now relegated to the annals of history. One of the regrets I had in later life was that I never questioned either Lionel or Colonel Westmacott more deeply about their past. I had missed the opportunity to be given a first-hand account of the lives people lived when the Empress-Queen Victoria ruled over one quarter of the world's population.

After hitch-hiking down to the southern tip of Malaya I prepared to cross from Johor to the newly independent city-state of Singapore. While waiting I became aware of a young British soldier about my own age.

The one-pip 2nd lieutenant was issuing orders to a platoon of soldiers who were manoeuvring a military vehicle onto a small pontoon ferry. He seemed so full of confidence, so imbued with his entitlement to command, so convinced that the world contained two kinds of people: those born to lead and those born to follow.

The contrast was painful. Had I worked harder at school and been more focused perhaps I would have been sent to this part of the world. Perhaps I would be confidently in command rather than hitchhiking which was after all, a form of begging.

Such thoughts were quickly swept aside when on

arrival in Singapore, I used a strategy learned from Klaus. Commandeering a taxi to go to the YMCA I negotiated at length with the owner of a vehicle that could accommodate six people. Then telling others who were standing around where the vehicle was going I sold individual places. The net result was a free ride into town.

In Singapore I made contact with a school friend, Tom Baines who at the age of seventeen, had left school with six "O" levels and joined the RAF. It seemed to me that one minute Tom was at school and the next he was an RAF officer. Within a couple of years of basic and officer training, he had been commissioned as the youngest Pilot Officer in the Royal Air Force. Tom was amazed and delighted to hear from me and we hastily planned a night out together.

Thinking ahead, I knew that a colleague from the food company in England was now based at their offices in New Delhi. Wanting the address of that office I visited the British food company's Singapore office. There I was greeted warmly by Benedict, a former management trainee whom I had not met before.

In his late 20s, Benedict was typical of young, expatriate managers living in Far Eastern cities. From an upper middle-class family he had been to public school and spoke with an impeccable accent. Despite his rather formal, perhaps even shy demeanour, he immediately took me out for lunch in a top-notch hotel. Benedict obviously enjoyed meeting me as I was able to update him with company gossip and the movements of some of his friends.

As we were leaving the restaurant, Benedict was greeted with a lovely smile by a beautiful Chinese woman. Instead of reacting warmly to her he seemed embarrassed and made no attempt at an introduction.

Having detected an intimacy from the woman I asked Benedict who she was. His deliberately vague and non-committal response was, 'Just some woman.'

I reflected on what that relationship might have been; they were both young, attractive and looked really good together. Were they lovers who had separated? Had there been infidelity and hurt?

At that time, was it considered inappropriate for an expat Englishman to have a Chinese lover? Was she perhaps a high-class courtesan about whom Benedict wished to remain discreet?

Benedict said he had plenty of space in his bungalow and invited me to stay with him. He even arranged for his driver to move my rucksack from the YMCA. I immediately 'phoned Klaus who was staying at the less expensive Chinese YMCA and asked if he would like to take over the Orchard Road YMCA room for which payment had already been made.

Klaus sounded very impressed that someone had lent me a car and was bowled over when he found out that the car came equipped with a driver.

Benedict returned home quite late that evening and said he had been driving his racing car. I assumed he meant some kind of clapped-out old sports car and was amazed when he showed me a photograph of a single-seat cigar-shaped car which genuinely looked like a scaled–down version of the sort of thing that Fangio and Stirling Moss were driving at the time.

Almost as a throwaway line, and without cracking a smile, Benedict said, 'I would let you drive it... but I hear you attract swinging weights.' Oh shit - I thought: cannot even escape that stupidity halfway round the world.

After pausing Benedict went on, 'You know, that business really upset Sir John.' 'Yes I know,' I said. 'I can understand he would be outraged by my abuse of a company car.'

Then Benedict's face broadened into a smile. 'Oh no, it wasn't that. Sir John was upset because he had been watching the event unfold from his fourth floor executive office. What really annoyed him was that he lost his bet with Jonathan, the MD.

Sir John, who as you know owns a few race horses and loves a flutter, had a tenner on you, reckoning you would make it.'

Over the next couple of days, when the car was available, I had the opportunity to travel around Singapore Island. On the weekend Benedict took me waterskiing in a beautiful palm-fringed inlet. Several of his friends were there, two of whom had their own boats.

Most Englishman of Benedict's age had been required to undertake National Service. With their privileged background these men had all been commissioned. One man, who had presumably stayed on for an extra year or two, reached the rank of Captain in the prestigious "Horse Guards."

I had purchased a new shirt to wear while socialising with Benedict's affluent friends, but my limited wardrobe was shabby in comparison to theirs. These beautiful, imperturbable young men and women were dressed casually but tastefully.

They exuded self-belief and entitlement, a by-product of their gilded lives, families' connections and "old money". They were all courteous and pleasant to me but I felt inadequate, knowing I was way out of my league. I had neither the confidence nor the ability to join in their banter and felt the occasion to be more of a strain than fun.

To my extreme embarrassment and annoyance Benedict told the assembled group about my encounter with the swinging weights. They roared with laughter, especially about Sir John losing his bet. With all eyes on me I felt compelled to respond in some way, so I blurted out, 'It's all right for you Benedict, you've got a racing car. Maybe I could have done it with that?'

Everyone laughed again as they raised their glasses in a mock toast. Benedict's guest was no longer boringly monochrome but sufficiently eccentric and offbeat to be of interest.

Tom contacted me saying he and two of his fellow junior officers were going to a party in Nee Soon the following evening and that I might like to join them. What he failed to mention was that neither he nor his friends, had actually been invited. On arrival we were the only people wearing anything other than a toga which made it pretty obvious we were gatecrashers. So, somewhat crestfallen we returned to town seeking other amusement.

Chatting over beer with Tom we caught up on each other's news and discussed mutual friends. Then, deciding to go on a Singaporean version of a pub crawl the group set off for the notorious Bugis Street with its parade of "women."

I had never heard of, let alone seen ladyboys before. Dressed elegantly as women some of them were very beautiful in their strapless, ankle-length pencil dresses.

One hand nonchalantly placed on a narrow hip while standing with their weight on the back foot gave their body a flattering line. Their mannerisms and gait so carefully studied and feminine made it hard to believe they had a middle wicket.

The drinking started in earnest as we went by

rickshaw from one brothel to another enjoying a beer in each place while the mama-sans introduced a parade of women. Our pretentiously louche attitude made it all too apparent we had no intention of availing ourselves of the services on offer in these depressingly seedy places.

'Let's get something to eat,' said one of the men. 'I know a great fish restaurant. It has a really funny sign outside which reads, "All our waitresses have freshly caught crabs which they are itching to pass on to you."'

After visiting about the fourth bordello I said something really stupid and derogatory. I don't remember exactly what, but it was to the effect that the women were all so unattractive I would need to be seriously pissed to shag any of them.

As if from the wings of a stage, a wiry little man shrieking like a banshee came charging out at great speed directly towards us wielding a heavy club. Instinctively all four of us leapt to our feet and rushed out of the door. The mama-san was obviously used to drunken men and knew exactly how to have them ejected.

Tom and his two friends were unimpressed by the embarrassing commotion I had caused. On reflection I realised it wasn't so much my bad behaviour, it was that three healthy young military types and a civilian had been terrified by one small Oriental man.

Although the Air Force obviously fights differently to the Army, this could perhaps have been a good lesson in tactics and bluff. Anyway, the net result was that the other two men were annoyed by me and went off on their own.

Unable to remember what I had actually said, Tom and I sat on a dilapidated wooden balcony in the old quarter of town drinking more beer. We looked down on the bustling marketplace, our nostrils filled with the smoke from charcoal braziers. Open cooking pots steamed and bubbled beneath us creating a scene which had changed little over the generations.

Having drunk far too much I accepted Tom's invitation to return with him and sleep in the Officers' quarters at RAF Seletar. Head spinning, I was aware that I should be staying with Benedict but thought to myself I was being free-spirited and independent; I did not have to check-in with anybody.

Understandably Benedict was upset the next day. He felt responsible for me and knew only that I had not returned home that night. I had abused the courtesy which had so generously been extended to me.

It was now no longer comfortable for me to remain as Benedict's guest so I volunteered to leave before being asked to. Like a fish that had been in the sun too long, Benedict's driver returned me to the very place from which he had collected me a few days earlier.

My head was throbbing and my throat dry, but the hangover wasn't the real problem. I felt utterly adrift and stupid; I had upset both the people who had extended the hand of friendship. Like a wine glass falling onto a tile floor, my newly acquired confidence shattered.

There was no one to whom I could turn even for silent support; terrible feelings of isolation and loneliness overwhelmed me. My carefree adventure had come off the rails and it was entirely my fault. I had confused the freedom of an independent traveller with social decency.

Worse still, instead of continuing to enjoy and appreciate the simple beauty and exoticism of the Far East I had been offensive to the local people. I behaved selfishly and had caused hurt and embarrassment to others. My selfish and unpleasant behaviour had gone far beyond the simple philosophy of expanding my boundaries.

Yes, I had set out to change some aspects of my personality but this was not the person I wanted to be. I had lost track of my core values, becoming arrogant and abusive in the process.

A phrase from Joseph Conrad's story of failure echoed in my mind. It was from "Lord Jim" his story of the English merchant navy officer who, when his ship was sinking during a terrible storm, shamefully abandoned his passengers to certain death. The phrase, which kept coming to my mind was.

'Who amongst us has not begged God for a second chance?' If only I could turn back the clock and undo the stupidity and damage.

Chapter 13

THE TURNING POINT

I was half-heartedly picking at a late-afternoon meal of mutton satay with rice in a local street market, the type of food stall where you simply sat at any table regardless of who else was there. Despite the fact that other tables were free I was joined in the shade by an interesting looking couple in their mid 50s, Dara Smedly and his Indonesian wife Pikki.

Dara, whom I was later to learn operated a small trading company, was wearing an ethnic shirt from the northern hill-tribe area of Thailand. On most Westerners this would have looked like an affectation but on Dara with his long, wavy, silver-grey hair it was not out of place.

Moreover, being with an oriental woman dressed in a local-weave reddish-brown, ankle-length skirt, allowed his appearance to blend harmoniously.

Shoulders hunched and looking down I was despondent and miserable. How could I have been so stupid, to let myself degenerate from being happy and upbeat to sad and dejected? My buoyancy and optimism had evaporated. The problem is that when we are depressed we can see no end to it. The depression itself is exacerbated by the expectation that we shall remain in this state forever.

My preference would have been to eat alone and I made no attempt to look up or engage them in any way. Dara initiated the conversation by asking what I was doing in Singapore. There were other superficial questions to which I grunted minimal responses. It was only on learning he was fluent in Hindi and a couple of other oriental languages that I became more interested. Having been born in India, Dara had spent most of his working career, including the war years, as an officer in the Indian Army.

Dara and Pikki had met 15 years ago in Surabaya, each recognising immediately that they had found a kindred spirit. Pikki was surprisingly fluent in English, explaining later that although she had never travelled outside Southeast Asia, she read extensively in English.

It was Pikki who suggested I might like to visit their home, which they rented from the Singapore government. It was she said, one of the few remaining old colonial houses, the type most expatriates spoke of with a romanticised affection and admired from the outside but declined to live in, because they were un-modernised and lacked air conditioning.

Regaining a modicum of curiosity I overcame my misgivings and accepted the offer. After a short walk we turned onto an avenue of fine, similarly-styled but nevertheless individual properties, each set within generous but simple grounds.

The similarity arose from the fact that every house was surrounded by a veranda on the lower level and many had an enclosed walkway on the upper level. These ensured that very little sunlight reached any of the windows.

The Smedley's house was neither the grandest nor the least impressive on the road. Rather, like its occupants, it sat comfortably and inconspicuously among its neighbours.

Entering through a high arched portico, my eyes had to adjust from sunlight to what seemed like semi-darkness. The house had a monastic feel, there was a calm, spiritual ambiance. Its slatted, plantation-style shutters kept out most of the light while permitting an unhurried breeze.

Dara put on a record of hauntingly emotional music. It was, he told me, sung by a popular Batak folk singer Gordon Tobing, renowned throughout his native Indonesia for the achingly beautiful timbre of his tenor voice.

Dara who had guided the conversation over the meal now withdrew to an adjoining room to study a large, illustrated volume depicting the Buddhist temples of Bagan.

Pikki and I moved to the shady veranda, scented by the fragrance of two large orange-jasmine plants. We chatted casually about Indonesia, as well as the journey I was on. She mentioned coming originally from Bali, "The Island of Gods."

Although a part of Indonesia it was, she said, quite different to the rest of the country. The people were imbued with a deep sense of spirituality woven from the strands of many religions.

She described the temples, garlanded carvings of deities, and long colourful streamers fluttering on the wind. The beauty of the centuries-old, man-made rice terraces climbing high into cloudless skies. Her description was of a flower-strewn paradise inhabited by people whose lives were ordained by their mysticism.

Why were you sad when we came to your table?' She asked gently. Her question so quietly asked that it was neither rude nor invasive: more an invitation to unburden whatever was troubling me.

Dispensing with my normal reticence which seemed

unnecessary in this refuge, I mumbled inarticulately.

'Don't really know. Just seem to be going through a bad time.' There was a long pause before she asked, 'What would you like to do to make it a better time?

Then it was I who was slow to respond. 'Don't really know,' I repeated, 'would just like to stop making mistakes and doing stupid things.

When pressed as to what mistakes I had made I told her I was feeling bad about my abuse of Benedict and Tom. Then there was the evening with Tom. It was not so much getting drunk as the fact that I had abused women whose lives were already wretched enough. I was showing off in front of my friend, trying to be clever. I felt guilt and embarrassment at the arrogance and disdain I had displayed. Not only that previous night but also in my immature behaviour when leaving Prayed in Bangkok. Again, abusing someone who had done so much for me.

'It seems to me,' I said, 'I have lost my way. I do not like the person I have become. If I am no longer an up-tight middle-class Englishman, then what am I? Just another self-centred Westerner enjoying these beautiful countries but giving nothing in return.'

As the floodgates opened I told Pikki about having won and lost Claire and that I might well be in the process of doing the same with Dagmar. What is wrong with a man who runs away from what he actually wants most, who is constantly looking for greener pastures?

Worst of all I had rejected and discarded the person I was, without having found a satisfactory replacement. Pikki did not rush to respond. She waited until I fully discharged, allowing the emotional pressure to dissipate. Although my eyes were downcast she looked softly at me and said. 'Throughout life, we constantly encounter setbacks. They give us the opportunity to learn. If we do not make mistakes it is because we are standing still and making no progress.

The key to benefiting from our mistakes is to acknowledge them. 'It is through the acceptance of our mistakes that we grow. What we gain is the wisdom that prepares us for the remainder of our lives. It is a double loss when we are defeated by our mistakes and deny them.

The greatest lesson we can take is to be open to doing things differently. To be flexible, adaptable, and above all to be resilient.'

She paused allowing me to absorb and mull over the things she had said. She was a person whom I had only just met and in all likelihood would never see again. That gave both of us enormous freedom. She could give me the message she felt I needed and I was at liberty to accept it or reject it.

'You are at the start of your adult life; acknowledge and be grateful for the gifts you have received. Be grateful to all those people who have helped you get to where you are. When we think about our parents and other people who have guided us, we must think positively about what they have given us.

'Life is about finding balance. We cannot be so cautious that we never risk anything or so reckless that we jeopardize that which we are unwilling to lose. We cannot be so fearful that we avoid new situations or so gullible we are endangered.'

Pikki then excused herself, ostensibly to ask Dara if he was ready for his usual late afternoon glass of ginseng-ginger infusion. I heard her speaking to him but she returned shortly, once again sitting down and continuing.

'Many people in this part of the world believe in the concept of Karma. The process whereby our lives are affected directly in response to our own actions. Christianity has its own version of this, expressed in the saying, "As ye sow, so shall ye reap."

'You, Paul, have been blessed with so much in life. You are physically healthy, intelligent and attractive. You can squander those gifts or you can use them. What you do with your gifts is for you to decide.'

Pikki told me I was undertaking something similar to that which was required of young men in parts of Sumatra. They were expected to leave the comfort and security of their home and to fend for themselves. They had to learn independence and to provide for themselves in every aspect of their lives.

They would find happiness and encounter hardship and sorrow. They would experience the pleasures of success as well as the pain and shame of failure.

Ideally, they would become wise in the ways of the world and would be reshaped on the anvil of experience. They would be hardened and tempered like the blade of a kris, into an object of strength and beauty.

When the time was right they would return to their home, changed from the boy who left into a man who is self-assured, assertive and ready to contribute.

For the first time, they would truly appreciate their families and recognise the merits and beauty of their own kampong.

'This undertaking,' said Pikki, 'is called Merantau. You, Paul, are doing Merantau.'

Standing behind my chair resting her hands on my shoulders, I revelled in the warmth of human touch and connection. My breathing stuttered into short jerky gasps as I struggled to draw air. Unbidden by me, a few tears made their own decision to descend my cheeks as Pikki's gifts of absolution and catharsis overwhelmed me.

Chapter 14

PENANG

Physically and metaphorically a turning point had been reached. Physically I would be retracing my steps back over the Malay border and travelling northwards. Emotionally I felt like a pendulum that having reached one extreme, was now hovering for that millisecond before returning in the opposite direction.

What I wanted was impossible; to hold that position, to remain in the no-man's-land of time, to pause and re-evaluate. To ask myself why I was travelling and what I was trying to achieve.

The train journey up the Malay Peninsular to the Penang crossing was uneventful, or perhaps it was merely that I failed to make my usual observations. I thought only about what Pikki had said and the wisdom of Merantau.

Reaching the YMCA in Penang proved to be a much-needed boost. I was delighted that the cost of the bed was a mere single Malay ringgit per night. More importantly I was happy to find many old friends and acquaintances, including Klaus.

Dear old Fuller was there, still wearing his baggy shorts and faded shirt. He was sitting at a table in the corner writing letters with his prized, black lacquer De La Rue fountain pen.

I chose to sleep on the cool, upper-balcony peering

up at the stars. Looking at the night sky is both wonderful and humbling. The vastness and beauty of the unfathomable universe. But I also chuckled remembering the satirist Peter Cook, who joked. 'As I looked out into the night sky, across all those infinite stars, it made me realise how insignificant they are.'

At night, or when I was out, I would leave my camera and other valuables in a locked room belonging to a crusty old Englishman. This chap had been a rubber-plantation manager in central Malaya until Chinese businessmen had taken over and dismissed him.

Now he was just another piece of human flotsam drifting around Southeast Asia. Unlike Fuller, he sadly no longer maintained the standards of his past.

Unshaven and unkempt the formerly proud man was now reduced to a battered, empty shell. Decades in the tropics and the circumstances of life had disconnected the man from his roots, leaving him without a family, a home or a base to which he could return.

I became friendly with a young Californian who had been working on a kibbutz in Israel. Together we visited the island's tropical gardens, enjoying the frenzied antics of the monkeys. In the intense, steamy heat we slid down a riverbank and taking off our shoes sat on a rock, dangling our feet in the wonderfully cool water. Children of all ethnicities, Malays, Indians and Chinese, uninhibited by their nakedness played happily around us in this veritable garden of Eden.

Despite everyone staying at the "Y", being in some way unique and different there was one Englishman who defied quick classification. In his late 20s perhaps, he was undernourished even by the standards of travellers and differentiated still further by his unusual shaven head.

Duncan had been a theological student in Lichfield, but had since transferred his philosophical interest to Buddhism. He was now en route to Thailand where he thought it possible that he would become a Buddhist novice. All of us referred to him as "Dunc the Monk" and joked he probably had a brother called "Kev the Rev". He was interested to hear of my time in Bangkok living in the monastery with Prayed. When I told him that my friendship had been marred by a request for money, Duncan looked horrified.

'Oh' he said with a hurt expression on his face, 'you got it wrong, you misunderstood completely. Prayed was not trying to extort money but was offering you the chance to receive spiritual benefit through the act of giving.'

Oh God! - I thought. Not only had I been rude but I had been rude and ignorant: a terrible combination of traits which I would try to avoid in future.

That evening Duncan and I walked together until finding a set of wooden steps leading down to a small, slow-flowing stream where we sat in the semi- darkness and chatted.

'As a Buddhist monk,' I said, 'you will get very little food and that is mostly plain rice. You do not have any money of your own and worst of all, as Prayed told me you could never touch a woman.

'Prayed' I said, 'willingly submitted to the harsh conditions and discipline of temple life and yet he was one of the most joyful and happy people I have met. Why is it that I, who am free to do anything I want, feel restless and dissatisfied?'

Duncan responded, 'You are not the first person to be restless and you will not be the last. The Buddha himself asked this same question 2500 years ago.

'The first thing to remember is that the man whom we now call the Buddha, was just that. He was a man and not a God. He had no supernatural powers and no desire to be worshipped. He developed a philosophy, a way in which life can yield the greatest overall happiness. The wonder of this philosophy lies in its simplicity.

'It merely recommends ideas with which we probably all agree anyway. It is that we should lead a moral life, we should be consciously aware of our thoughts and actions and that we should pursue ever greater knowledge and wisdom.'

Just as Duncan was getting into his treatise I did a very non-Buddhist thing. I swatted a mosquito that had punctured my left forearm. Knowing that Buddhists would not kill any living creature it seemed as if I owed him an apology.

'Sorry Duncan,' I said, 'but quite apart from the fact that I do not like mosquitoes draining my arteries, I'm doing everything possible to protect myself from malaria and dengue fever.'

Ignoring both my summary execution of the mosquito and apology Duncan carried on. 'People describe Buddhism as a religion. If by that they mean belief in an all-controlling power whom they can petition to intercede on their behalf, then the term religion is not applicable to Buddhism.

'But,' I said 'I have seen many people in Buddhist temples praying to the Buddha. If the Buddha is not a God then to whom do they pray and for what purpose? Moreover, if Buddhists pray and gain benefit, then so too can anyone including agnostics and atheists.'

'The answer,' said Duncan, 'is that Buddhists believe in an abstract principle of goodness. They believe that people form their own concept of God in a less formalised way than in a religion such as Christianity.

It is somewhat circular in that the listener or recipient, is the same person who is praying. It is a form of meditation - a cleansing of the mind which removes negativity and concentrates on positive thoughts.'

That made far greater sense to me than the dogma and inflexibility of the Abrahamic religions. Moreover, it was apparent that one could practise the philosophy and reap the benefits of Buddhism while still believing wholeheartedly in Darwinism.

Concluding, Duncan said, 'To learn Zen, we have to be at one with nature; to flow as water flows. The message that Zen gives us, is that it is up to each of us to find our own happiness.'

Feeling more positive and relaxed I thanked Duncan and wished him well on his journey of spiritual exploration.

In the letter which Duncan would take Prayed I started by telling him how enjoyable and inspirational it had been to meet him. Remembering our trip on the Chao Prya river I told him the laughter we shared on that occasion would be an abiding memory. I thanked him for his support and hospitality.

Finally, I said what I really wanted to say. That was to apologise for my ignorance and rudeness, and ask for his forgiveness.

Writing to Dagmar but without going into detail, I told her about my experiences in the Malay Peninsula. All I said was that I had encountered ups and downs. Most of all, I told her how much I missed her.

Next I wrote sincere notes to Benedict and Tom, apologising for my shortcomings as their guest.

Benedict, despite his straight-laced exterior would be grateful for my letter and accept my apology. Tom would wonder why I had written such a wimpish letter about an incident already relegated to his archive of stories to be regurgitated in the Officers' mess.

I was trying to get a deck-class passage on a ship called the State of Madras from Penang to Madras. The authorities claimed not to like selling this lowest class of ticket to Europeans. So I had to visit many puffed- up petty officials, trying to buy the ticket I wanted.

Eventually I was told that they would be drawing lots for the remaining five tickets which were in high demand from a few Europeans and host of Indians.

Finally, displaying a head wiggle - which in England would have indicated 'no' but to Indians signified agreement - Mr. Jumabuoy the official in charge informed me I had been one of the lucky ones.

It is probable Mr. Jumabuoy had already decided I should have one of these tickets but kept me in suspense anticipating an urgent, last-minute donation of baksheesh.

As the ship was in port and ready to leave the following day I went out with my Californian friend and a young Swiss man. We enjoyed the camaraderie and laughed at the amazing offers of sexual service. One tout said we could have a man, a woman, a boy, a girl, or any type of animal we wished.

It reminded me of the joke in which an uptight Englishman in Egypt responded to similar offers by saying that he was outraged and wanted the British consul. The pimp replied that getting the British consul might be difficult but he would do his best.

Sometimes I responded to these shopping list offers of sexual service by specifying the only thing I would accept. In full knowledge that they would be unable to supply it in the Far East, I said I wanted a woman who was as tall as me.

The three of us wandered round the Chinese district of Penang doing what so many young men did. Drinking a few beers and fending off yet more fantastic propositions from pimps and rickshaw drivers.

In reference to Duncan, the Californian chap said he had a friend who used to be unemployed. But that has all changed now, he continued, 'He has taken up meditation. After all, it's better than sitting around all day doing nothing.'

To round off the evening we visited a couple of brothels, making it clear from the outset that we were only there for the ambience and the beer. Then, in cheerful mood, we raced our cycle rickshaws like Roman chariots until the poor men could peddle no more.

Chapter 15

THE "STATE OF MADRAS"

Catching first sight of the tired, weather-beaten ship named State of Madras, most Europeans would immediately be alarmed by her unsafe condition. Even tied up alongside the wharf she appeared to have a slight list.

Paint had not been wasted on her and she was in no way a vessel of beauty. The hull, which was predominantly a faded matt-black, exhibited random blotches of other colours. The superstructure which had originally been white, now displayed an infinite array of rust-coloured streaks.

None of this mattered to me as the ship represented another adventure. I was excited by the prospect of once again experiencing something totally new and different.

There were hundreds of predominantly ethnic Indian men, jostling to board the ship. Theoretically passengers were boarded by the number on their ticket. But these were Indians and no one took any notice of what they were told. I was bewildered as the human tide surged past me onto the ship.

Bewilderment changed to annoyance when a large, very rotund Sikh urgently pushed past. His bulk was such that, unintentionally he pushed me off balance nearly causing me to fall off the narrow, bouncy gangplank.

Catching sight of my purple ticket but without slowing his pace, the Sikh pulled me by the upper arm, shouting: 'Come! Come!' Understanding this was no time for gentlemanly restraint I joined the unstoppable flow boarding the ship.

The amount of luggage each person had with them was indicative of their affluence. The poorest having little more than a folded square of cloth containing their meagre possessions. Others lugged heavy, over-stuffed, rattan bags like those I had seen being made by old women in the markets.

Class turned out to be an important issue on this floating village. There were the usual, first and second classes, which together accommodated 100 people. But the State of Madras had one lower class nominally called "un-berthed" but realistically known as deck- class.

These 1000 passengers, which included me, were quite literally confined to using the open deck at the stern of the ship. There was little or no protection from the elements, including the glaring tropical sun. For all this, I could think of nothing more enjoyable than sleeping in the open and looking up at the stars.

The Sikh, who appeared to know the procedure, threw his bedding onto the deck. 'You put here,' he commanded, indicating a patch of space beside his own. When I placed my things neatly in a small space, the Sikh gesticulated and shouted at me, 'Make bed space.'

Realising that there was a requirement to claim sufficient territory on which to sleep, I commandeered a patch about 6 feet long by 3 feet wide. The top was secure against a bulkhead and one side was impenetrably defended by the voluminous presence of the Sikh. As passengers scrambled to establish themselves, my space was inevitably eroded on the two undefended perimeters.

It did cross my mind that should the Sikh roll over during the night it would have the same effect as being flattened by a steamroller. I also laughed to myself, remembering the analogy a woman had used to describe her extremely large husband making love to her. She said, 'It was like having an enormous wardrobe fall on top of her - but with the key still in the lock.'

In the evening, when all the passengers were on board and starting to calm down, the crew took in the hawsers and allowed the ship to slip out to sea on the retreating tide to start our five day voyage. There was no fanfare and no crowds of relatives waving goodbye. Although the passengers looked very different to those on the Sylvania, there was once again a strong sense of excitement mingled with trepidation.

Perhaps that is the very nature of important journeys. We travel optimistically from what is known towards that which we are seeking, all the while apprehensive that our plans could falter.

Of the hundreds of people on this overcrowded, patently unsafe ship, only eight were Caucasians. In addition to me there was Ron a New Zealander, five American Peace Corps workers travelling second-class and an English woman in first-class.

There was a primitive sort of cafeteria for the use of deck-class passengers. It was disgustingly dirty: stale water and garbage slopped backwards and forwards along the clogged drainage ducts. The meals they dispensed were totally repulsive, consisting of tongue-blisteringly spicy vegetarian curry served on rusting metal plates. One of the servers searched to find a spoon or fork for me. The implement he returned with was so abhorrently filthy I chose to eat with my fingers like everyone else.

One meal consisted of a ball of soggy, glutinous rice. A creature which looked like a small shrimp bravely fought its way out of the top, climbed down the rice ball and walked across my plate. Then it wandered over the table before falling to the floor. Ron who had witnessed this incident said nothing, but pushed his own plate away.

The Tamil server wore only a heavily stained, grease saturated towel. During our conversation he picked his nose and with the bogey still hanging from his finger, used that hand to pass a chapati to me. For some reason I do not think that place will ever be awarded a Michelin star. Unsurprisingly, I ate little on the journey other than the bananas, oranges and biscuits I had brought with me.

With the eating facilities in that condition, it was no surprise to find the squat lavatories to be visually abhorrent and olfactorily repugnant. Lavatories in the developing world can cause even the most travel-hardened to recoil at their sulphurous, rotten-egg stench, but the actual smell differs according to the prevailing diet.

Here the obnoxious, rancid curry odour could be detected in most parts of the ship, but was sometimes partially obscured by the ubiquitous and preferable smell of bunker-oil and engine smoke.

During the daytime the decks were a seething mass of bored Indians, all dressed identically in traditional off-white peasant dhotis and shawls.

Looking like a flock of Mahatma Gandhis they would chat amongst themselves in Hindi or Urdu while smoking 'beedis', the cheap Indian cigarettes made from the poorest quality tobacco wrapped in Coromandel leaves.

Sometimes someone would saunter to the side of the ship to spit out a gelatinous glob of red betel. On a sufficient number of occasions the sputum-like material thus produced would be returned unwanted by the wind, adding to the red stains on the gunwales.

At night every inch of deck space, as well as both open holds, were covered by rows of bodies so tightly packed it resembled a slave ship. In the mornings there was a long queue for the single tap under which I could undertake only the most modest of ablutions.

There was a small awning over the area where I lay, but on the two occasions when it rained this afforded little protection. The rain not only travelled horizontally underneath it, but as the ship rolled, a small ripple of water slid rhythmically, from side to side across the deck.

Even on dry nights I woke frequently, turning over to relieve the pain generated in my bony hips. The thin rattan mat I had hastily acquired for the voyage gave little relief from the hardwood deck.

At night I covered myself with an increasingly soiled camel coat which had travelled with me from England. While far from being a Savile Row garment, it had at one time been moderately fashionable and good enough to wear in town.

Incongruous though this coat was in the tropics, I had decided to keep it as a sort of wearable sleeping bag. I was pleased to have it with me now and glad to have carried it around in the ancient straw bag Klaus had picked up in Cambodia.

Travelling in first-class was a party of lively female students, some Chinese some Malay. They, together with their teachers, which included the English lady, were all from the prestigious Victoria Institute in Kuala Lumpur.

The girls, one of whom I was told was a Tunku (daughter of a state ruler and therefore a sort of princess) had their own small private piece of deck. This looked down on the aft-deck where I spent most of my time. Once or twice I had seen a couple of girls looking in my direction and giggling.

On a few occasions after that, one of the girls would call down and invite me to come up and join them. I would never have dreamt of going up without an invitation, but enjoyed my visits. Chatting with them broke the monotony of my day, as well as theirs.

I was fascinated by and attracted to many of these girls, who joked and laughed constantly in a delightfully infectious way. At the same time I was aware of what I considered to be an enormous age gap. I was 21 and the girls were only 17 or 18.

The Sikh who had befriended me from the start of the voyage, had introduced himself as Jangjeet, saying that his name meant, 'One who conquers the battlefield of the mind.' We remained allies and companions, looking after each other's belongings.

Sitting cross-legged on the deck in the late afternoon heat chatting to Jangjeet, I thought of Dagmar and knew she would roar with laughter if she could have seen me.

That thought was interrupted when one of the ship's officers appeared and said the captain wished to see me. This felt like being summoned to the headmaster's office and I wondered what I had done wrong.

In contrast to the ship itself, the Indian captain, standing on the bridge, was impressive and impeccably turned out. His white trousers were fresh and crisply ironed; his immaculate white shirt had razor-sharp creases down the short sleeves.

He greeted me with a broad smile and a warm handshake, saying, 'Come this way.'

Sitting in the control room with its highly polished brass fittings he produced a bottle of Johnnie Walker Red and without asking, filled a tumbler to a generous three fingers and handed it to me.

The captain proudly showed me a brass plate indicating the ship had been built by Swan Hunter of Tyneside in 1947, but that its original name had been Jaljawahar. He was amiable and asked me where I was going and what I was doing, totally bemused by the fact that a well mannered and apparently upper-class Englishman should wish to travel in this fashion.

Everyone he knew, and certainly every English gentleman he had ever met, would do everything possible to avoid travelling in such squalor and discomfort. Perhaps it was for this reason, and out of curiosity that he had summoned me. Although I declined a second drink my tumbler was refilled anyway.

The anaesthetic effect of the first undiluted drink was such that the second appeared to sting less. The combination of dehydration, lack of food and too much Scotch gave me a woozy head and rubbery legs. It was with much difficulty and deliberate concentration I negotiated the steep, ship's ladder-stairs and found my way back to the stern.

The ship provided little in the way of entertainment for its flock of deck-class sheep. Rigging up a large sheet one night, the crew projected an Indian movie. Its lack of a sound track did nothing to dampen everyone's enthusiasm.

Greater entertainment was provided the next day by a man who became trapped in one of the lavatories. His eventual release from incarceration was witnessed and cheered by almost everyone on the ship from the captain down.

On the fourth day I was told the girls would be putting on a variety show in the first-class lounge that evening. When I received an invitation to attend directly from the captain I was elated.

The first thing that went through my mind was that I would have a wonderful meal in first-class before the entertainment. I visualised all the mouth-watering food that would be served and started to salivate at the prospect.

Then came the bad news. I was to join the first- class passengers in the lounge at 8.30 P.M. - after dinner!

Having paid off the attendant in second-class, I was able to use the washroom to clean up and shave. Looking in the mirror I realised how suntanned my face had become. Stupidly I had never purchased or worn a hat and the skin on my face was dry and leathery.

I put on the crumpled white shirt I had purchased in Singapore and proceeded to my important rendezvous. Most of the passengers were already in place. Looking around the back of the room I could not see a vacant chair.

'Here, here,' shouted the Captain as he ushered me to a large, padded and very comfortable armchair next to his in the front row, which appeared to have been saved for me. Again, without asking he poured a substantial shot of Johnnie Walker into a tumbler and handed to me.

I wondered why the Captain took an interest in me. Boredom perhaps? After all, for him this was just another of many voyages. Did he find it amusing to have an eccentric young English "gentleman" as his guest? Was there perhaps a subconscious feeling that he as an Indian was in charge, and under these circumstances superior to a representative of his former colonial masters?

When asked why the captain had singled me out for attention instead of one of the other Caucasians, such as Ron or the Peace Corps workers, Jangjeet seemed surprised. 'Oh,' he said 'it is because although you are un-berthed everyone knows you are a pukka sahib.'

All the Victoria Institute girls were barefoot and dressed in brightly coloured Baju Karung, the traditional Malay costume. These are ankle-length skirts with a complimentary, form-fitting long-sleeve blouse which reached to the top of their hips, accentuating their nubile young curves. The uniformly slim, happy and playful schoolgirls had metamorphosed into young women of heart-stopping beauty and femininity.

An ancient wind-up gramophone blared out lively, up-tempo folk music. Unable to recognise the instruments being played the Captain informed me that they were mostly plectrumed instruments. When combined with a couple of bamboo flutes they were collectively known as rondalla.

A group of the girls performed a Filipino "tinikling" bamboo dance. This consisted of a girl holding the ends of two thick eight-foot-long bamboos. Another girl picked up the other two ends, and holding them about eighteen inches apart they started to bang the bamboos rhythmically on the floor.

Using them as percussive instruments, the rhythm was enhanced to include banging the bamboos together. So there were two rapid taps to the ground, followed by one when the bamboos struck together.

Two dancers then joined in, stepping quickly in and out of the bamboos before they clapped together. It was quite an exciting spectacle as there was always the risk of a girl getting her ankle hit between the two bamboos. Then two more girls with two more bamboos knelt beside the first two. Four dancers now had to move from one side to the other, carefully timing their rapid steps to the same rhythm. I was mesmerised by the intricacy of the dance and enchanted by the girls.

The dances were each given an introduction, as were the songs sung by individuals or small groups. As the lights were dimmed one of the girls came out to explain the next dance we were about to see.

'We perform for you a dance called Diya,' she said. 'It is an Indonesian folkloric story of a girl who lost her engagement ring and had to search for it until late at night, using a candle on a plate. She had to bend low to the ground and twist around.'

Three girls started to dance: in each hand they held a saucer-like dish containing a short, flickering candle. Moving slowly to the hypnotic, gong-chime, gamelan-style music, they gracefully moved their arms in circular movements above their heads. They also turned their hands under their outstretched arms, all the while being careful not to upset or extinguish the candles.

Finally they positioned themselves behind each other at different heights, moving their arms up and down in such a way as to create an eerie reincarnation of the six-armed Hindu Goddess, Kali.

Fear bordering on terror overwhelmed me. Where was I? What was happening? As if drugged I was totally disoriented and frightened by my own inability to comprehend my circumstances.

Trying to focus in the darkness I was bewildered, perplexed. Unbalanced and alarmed, the only thing I could see was a shaft of light coming through a window.

But the light itself, the window, and indeed where I was, remained a mystery until a few moments later when I realised...

This was the empty first-class lounge in darkness, other than the light coming from the gangway outside. The last thing I could remember was the candle dance. Nothing after that. So presumably that is when I fell asleep.

"Oh God I thought, a deck class passenger who had slept through the remainder of the entertainment. Then, in the comfort of a large padded armchair carried on sleeping until the early hours of the morning.

Panic stricken I felt an urgency to flee the scene but my legs were unsteady from the Johnnie Walker and fatigue. The steps down from the upper level was steep and dew-slippery, causing me to stumble a couple of times.

Carefully I negotiated my way stepping over reams of sleeping bodies wrapped in their deathly looking white shrouds, before eventually finding the sanctuary of my own little strip of deck.

The following day I was too embarrassed to venture anywhere near the Victoria Institute girls. The sight of me slouched in deep sleep as the first-class passengers slowly emptied out of the lounge must have created some amusement, especially among the girls.

Looking through binoculars I caught my first sight of the Indian coast. It looked the way I would have expected an African shoreline to look, with two large encampments of darkly thatched huts set amid dry, featureless bush-land. Reaching the Coromandel coast, the ship anchored offshore near the town of Nagapatnam in Tamil Nadu State.

Arab-looking lateen-rigged dhows tacked their way

out to the ship in order to take off some passengers and allow others to board. Although the sea was relatively calm this proved to be a difficult business. The dhows bobbed up and down making it hazardous for the passengers to transfer themselves and their belongings.

The whole process was totally disorganised, with everyone shouting their advice. Those shouting the loudest were the passengers who were not themselves directly involved. Some of the baggage fell into the sea in what I came to recognise as typical Indian chaos.

On the fifth and final night of the voyage, I was, to my surprise, once again invited to the first-class lounge for the Farewell evening. Self-consciously I tried to slip into the lounge unobtrusively. But as I entered, the room fell silent and every pair of eyes locked onto me. In that instant I could not read the group's attitude towards me. Did they consider me to be a drunken freeloader?

Fortunately the ice was quickly broken by several of the girls who started clapping to welcome me. Within seconds everyone in the first-class lounge had joined in laughing and clapping. Thank heavens! - I thought: what a relief, they have forgiven me.

The ancient record player was again coaxed into action and some of the passengers started to dance. Many of the girls were dancing together and I wanted to join in, having my eye on one Chinese girl in particular.

She was not only very lively but also very attractive. We had spent a lot of time talking on deck and we now had a couple of dances together. This caused much amusement to the onlookers, mostly because of the difference in our height: she being little more than five foot and my being unusually tall.

After the singing of Auld Lang Syne, the Chinese girl

happily accepted my offer of a walk round the crowded, postage-stamp sized upper deck. She was practically crying and I realised that she was sad to think that we would be saying goodbye and that she would never see me again.

In turn I also became emotional and spontaneously planted a gentle little kiss on her tender lips. This was an innocent gesture but meaningful to us both: perhaps more important to the Chinese girl, for whom it could conceivably have been her first kiss.

The kiss was observed by one of the teachers who had been following us. Like an Edwardian chaperone she made her presence obvious. This annoyed me: I would never have acted improperly and genuinely liked this girl.

Early the following morning, before disembarkation could take place, customs officers boarded the ship looking for contraband. This struck terror into the hearts of many petty smugglers. Among these was Ron who was heavily laden with cheap watches. Some Indians were carrying contraband or dutiable items such as transistor radios and nylon shirts, both of which were recent technological innovations.

It was illegal to import rupees but obviously many of the passengers would have exchanged their last Malay ringgit for rupees prior to departure. I myself had hidden three Rs.100 notes inside my camera, which I then advanced to make it look as if it had film in it.

When questioned, all of the Peace Corps workers denied having any rupees. Safely through immigration, one of the customs officers jokingly said to a Peace Corps worker, 'How many rupees do you really have?'

In the spirit of good humour he admitted to having 400. The response from a suddenly un-smiling customs officer was an immediate demand for Rs.100 or he would be searched. Another lesson learned.

Footnote.

Two years later (November 1966) the Rajula, an almost identical sister ship to the "State of Madras" carrying just over 1300 passengers was on a voyage from Singapore to Madras.

At this time a massive tropical cyclone (hurricane) caused extensive damage in the Madras region. So severe, it blew the Rameshwaram passenger train off its tracks. The Rajula sought refuge in Nagapattinam but was incredibly refused entry by the port authorities. The net result, was the most terrible ordeal for the ship, which tried to steam away from the coast but was continually swept back. As the ship rolled heavily, furniture piled up on the starboard side and windows shattered. Alarmingly, life rafts were blown overboard and its anchor chain severed.

Deck class passengers are said to have tied themselves to anything stable to avoid being thrown around as the ship plunged and rolled in high seas. After nearly running aground on several occasions the ship endured a further three days of appalling conditions before finally berthing safely in Madras.

Chapter 16

INDIA

My parents had lived in India for a decade but with Partition, and its unforeseen horrors looming, my parents decided to move back to England. After giving the matter much consideration, I resolved to go with them.

My third birthday was celebrated (if three-year-olds celebrate) while passing through the Suez Canal. In reality I had no memory of India but had subsequently seen so many pictures of my parents' time there it had created a sense of connection with the country.

Entering the Madras Immigration Office I looked much as you would expect of a man who had spent five nights, (well, four-and-a-half) sleeping on the deck of a ship. Despite my dishevelled, weather-beaten appearance, the smartly turned out young Immigration Officer looked at my passport and said with a smile, 'Welcome home, Sir.'

What a strange feeling. I did not feel worthy of his courtesy, nor did I feel this was my home. Seavale was my home... but because my parents had moved away it was unlikely I would ever live there again. So where did I belong?

By foot and in a shared trishaw, Ron and I headed straight for the YMCA. As soon as we had dumped our bags we rushed out to find a restaurant which claimed to serve Western style food. We ate and ate like the starving men we were, not allowing the irrelevance of conversation to impede our intake of food.

A couple of days later Ron left Madras and I went to see him off at the crowded railway station. In the process of saying farewell to Ron I met a tall, somewhat masculine American girl called Ruth who said she was looking for a hotel room. We toured around together viewing cheap accommodation until she found a room which she considered suitable.

Returning to the YMCA I spent several hours patiently changing the details of a student card I had been given in Penang by an Australian. When it was as good as I could make it, complete with a stamped photograph, I set off for the Concessions Office of the Indian Railways.

There, for the princely sum of 35 rupees, which in any case I had purchased on the black market in Penang, I acquired a student-discounted, third-class ticket. This was going to give me two days travel, complete with a sleeper and take me all the way to New Delhi.

The YMCA in Madras was housed in an old colonial building. My room, which at that time I had to myself, was laid out with a sleeping area separated from the rest of the room by an ornate, fret-work mahogany screen. Dozing on my bed one afternoon I became aware that the door opened slowly and silently.

A boy cautiously peered in before surreptitiously entering the room and walking towards the rupees sitting on a table. As soon as the boy spotted me he ran off. I pursued him shouting so loudly that he stopped only to provide an implausible excuse as to why he had entered the room.

Everywhere I went in India I was wary of being robbed. Stories circulated of people having their back pockets slit open on buses and would-be robbers slithering around, climbing over and jumping off any obstacle in order to steal from the unsuspecting.

Then there was the saga of an American who had his passport stolen. A few days later, when still frantically trying to work out what he would do, a deformed beggar crawled into his room with the passport. Although he claimed to have found it, and obviously expected a handsome reward for its return, the assumption was that he was merely being employed to undertake the delivery by the crooks who had stolen it.

A missing limb was by no means unusual in Madras. On more than one occasion when travelling by bus, I found a gnarled old leper would sit beside me. When walking alone, or with one of my Caucasian companions, I would hear the constant cry of, 'Master, Master.'

I was aware that many people here had to support an entire family on as little as three rupees a day. By comparison, I acknowledged my own high level of wealth. I too had been relatively poor in the midst of people who had so much more than me, but I had never suffered perpetual hunger and ongoing desperation.

For all this compassion I decided not to give to any more beggars, simply because there were too many, and giving to one merely increased the number of demands. Yet some of the sights I encountered were so abjectly pitiful my heart would not let me pass by. I understood that these people were begging not merely for food - they were begging for their very existence.

Jack, another New Zealander arrived at the YMCA and was put into the room with me. He said that using black market rupees he had purchased a passage from Madras to New Zealand. For some reason his passport had remained with an apparently questionable shipping agent in Bombay. To add to his worries Jack was obviously very sick, looking jaundiced and completely lacking any appetite.

When he was a little better, Jack, Ruth and I went out for dinner. Ruth told us her life story, which was heartbreakingly sad. It was not so much the appalling living conditions and physical abuse she had suffered, but the rejection by her foster parents which left her feeling isolated and lonely.

Such hardship would destroy most people, but not Ruth, who was street-smart and had realistic plans to set up an import-export business. I had nothing but admiration for her and felt sure she would one day become a successful business-woman.

Ruth taught me every currency trick she knew, which helped me avoid being cheated and to get the most advantageous exchange rates. For example, my funds were in different denomination US dollar travellers' cheques. Some moneychangers wanted large denomination cheques and notes and were willing to offer a better exchange rate for them. I could get 101 or even 102 $1 bills for a $100 travellers' cheque.

Similarly, I learned never to accept old, torn and soiled US dollar bills because they in turn would be difficult to pass on. The preference to carry and use clean banknotes was to remain with me for the rest of my life. Ruth also gave me detailed instructions on how to go about bribing people, although this is something I never did beyond the provision of a little baksheesh or "tea-money" as it was called.

Looking down from a second story window next evening, I saw a man climb up the side of a very small building, which turned out to be a lavatory. It became apparent that the man lived in this tiny area with just enough space to keep his few possessions and to lie down.

Where and how people slept in India was so different. People slept in doorways, on the pavements, and on simple benches. Seeing one man sleeping precariously on the narrow counter in a shop I thought it would be painful if he fell off. While night-time was the most obvious, there appeared to be no particular hours or routine for sleeping. People slept when and wherever they could.

Donating my old mat to the 'Y' I set off for the station. Fighting my way through the excited crowds, pushing down the aisle I found my designated wooden seat. After turfing-off a mud-encrusted labourer, I sat down thinking to myself that very few people in England would ever be lucky enough to have the experience of a two-day train journey across India while travelling in third class. It failed to cross my mind that the vast majority of people would not wish to have that experience anyway.

Every carriage contained three or four times the number of occupants for which it had been designed. People sat on the hard benches provided and also on the floor amidst their baggage. When the train pulled into a station they climbed over each other like puppies. New passengers, finding the doors blocked, simply threw their belongings through a window and scrambled in after them.

The train would announce its departure with an optimistic, ear-shattering horn-blast before struggling out of a station. The last teacups were then hastily snatched back by the chai-wallahs, the ubiquitous tea vendors who for the cost of a few annas had been dispensing their sugared, milky infusion. Passengers would start to unwrap banana leaf packages containing aromatic curry, dhal and chapatis. Even when passing through the desert, nothing was intentionally thrown out of the window.

While this was good for the landscape it did mean that the carriage was soon ankle-deep in fruit peel and curry stained banana leaves. As most of the passengers chewed areca nuts wrapped in betel leaves, the wooden walls inside the train had numerous blood-red blotches and streaks.

Being white and an oddity in this environment, every move I made was studied with obvious curiosity and I was never left in peace. Whenever one of the Indians could speak a little English he would interpret questions from the other passengers. I always told them that I had been born in India which pleased them just as it had the immigration officer in Madras. Despite this, none of the passengers could understand why I was not travelling in first class.

This prompted me to re-examine why I was undertaking this journey and why I was doing it under such adverse conditions. Why I was travelling, was the easier question to answer. I had known from the very start of my journey that I wanted to have excitement and new experiences. Travelling at the most basic level brought me into direct contact with people and circumstances which I was unlikely to encounter in any other way.

Moreover, as a child of both the frugal 50s and rectory life, doing things basically and inexpensively came naturally. If I ever travelled again in the future I hoped to be in a position to do it more comfortably, possibly even in luxury? Besides which I still had to negotiate my way back to England on the funds that remained and then take care of myself when I got there.

There was no thought of ever requesting any sort of assistance from my parents or anyone else. Anyway, my parents had only the vaguest idea where I was.

Had I been incarcerated or killed it might have taken weeks, possibly months before they even considered making enquiries.

Arriving at my next destination, the Uttar Pradesh town of Jhansi, was like returning to the middle ages with its seventeenth-century fortress dominating the arid, rocky hilltop. The narrow, fly-infested streets in which people worked outside their houses using methods of cooking, weaving and metal-beating unchanged for centuries.

Some of the men carried ancient rifles which I later learned were a status symbol, although I was also told they probably could not afford to fire them. Here no one spoke any English but they all knew where I was going. I, like any other outsider would be heading for the fabled temples of Khajuraho.

After a day bumping around on a variety of local buses I arrived at the tourist bungalow and asked for a bed. The proprietor, seeing my exhausted, bedraggled state, lied and said that he had no beds available, only a single room. I was so road-weary, the pores of my skin having been sealed with dust, that without argument I took the room.

The restorative powers of a shower did much for me and with renewed vigour I went into dinner. To my surprise and despite the odd assortment of clothes worn by the other guests, this was a relatively formal affair. An old bearer padded barefoot from table to table serving the meal.

Technically this was a four course meal, but everyone including me left the table still hungry. The bungalow manager obviously knew how to extract maximum revenue and deliver minimum service to people whom he never expected to see again. Fortunately, the following morning I was able to move into a communal room which I was to share with three other men.

After making these logistical arrangements, I set off to explore one of the fabled groups of temples. They were indeed remarkable, but despite their ornate, three-dimensional depiction of Kama Sutra sexual activity, I felt they were strangely soulless. Apart from a couple of sari-clad women whose scarves billowed in the wind, there were few other people there. For me, this was an environment that needed human energy and a jostling crowd.

Returning to the bungalow after having trekked for miles, I got into conversation with Callum, a British teacher who had been working in Africa. The first thing that struck me about this man was that his hair curled down to his shoulders. At that time and in Western cultures, hair that long was only associated with women.

The second remarkable thing about Callum was how articulate and knowledgeable he was. He had studied comparative religion and explained the reason for the Khajuraho depictions of virtually every known sex act performed in every possible position.

'These carvings,' he said, 'are at least 1000 years old - created during the century prior to the Norman invasion of England. Khajur,' he went on, 'means "date palm" and so we have been visiting the Date Palm Temples.

'There are differing theories as to why they were built. One explanation for the erotic carvings was that they taught religious devotees the ultimate self-control. They were constantly looking at an endless variety of sexual imagery depicting desirable scenarios in which they themselves would never participate.

'Another version told of a young widow who had

been ravished by the Moon God, leaving her pregnant. As this was unacceptable in her society she fled into the seclusion of nearby forests. The son to whom she gave birth grew up to become a powerful King who at his mother's behest, built the temples.

'Their carvings were designed to reveal and acknowledge the beauty and desirability of human passion and erotic fantasy.'

The old bearer who had served dinner the previous night padded past, and Callum catching his eye called out in Hindi requesting two glasses of lemon and mint. 'Delicious,' he said. 'Much more thirst quenching than tea I always think.' Then continuing his discourse, he said.

'Subsequently some Indian sects, especially those involved in Yoga, would combine the disciplines of physical and spiritual exercise in their pursuit of Nirvana. As Kama had been defined by some as the pursuit of pleasure, including sex, it was considered desirable. Some religious sects even required adherents to participate in Tantric rituals.'

Another guest in the Dak bungalow was a Dane who appeared to be in his late 20s, possibly thirtyish, but not substantially older than me. Yet to my amazement Soren said he was an assistant professor at Copenhagen University.

The very title Professor was daunting for me as I felt so academically inadequate. He spoke articulately in English, at times using words outside my vocabulary. Like Callum, he too appeared to be an expert on Asian and Oriental religions.

The two us talked late into the evening, and as we gained each other's trust, we exchanged personal stories. I told him about Mitsuko and the wonderful night we had spent together.

'Shinto' he said, 'recognises neither good nor evil. So the concept of personal guilt, especially that associated with sex in the West, does not exist for most people in Japan. Sex can be harmlessly shared and enjoyed just like any other personal interaction. Affection, attraction and romance are all natural and desirable facets of life, which may or may not be enhanced through sex.

'Rather than belief in a deity, love of nature and ritual are at the heart of Shinto. Japanese do not think of Shinto as a religion, but merely as one of many strands to their lives.

A philosophical outlook which can if they wish, run in parallel with a religion such as Buddhism. 'Unlike Catholicism, Shinto believes that people are naturally good. There is no sense of original sin or that human beings have in any way "fallen."

Cleansing of spirit and body through ritual bathing is significant in Shinto and that may be why Mitsuko was able to bathe with you so comfortably and naturally.

'Similarly, she expected you to bathe her to ensure equality and symmetry. Shinto trusts that through ritual, music and the pursuit of beauty, a state of calmness can overcome the general disorder of our lives.'

That night was the first time I had felt cold since leaving Alaska. As Indian hostelries of this type did not provide any bedding, I had taken down some of the rough, dusty curtains and laid them over my bed.

This amused two of the men now sharing my room. They were American Peace Corps workers with whom I was to form a valuable friendship. Clayton and Clive were tall, rangy-looking characters who dressed somewhat incongruously in jeans and cowboy boots, looking as if they had just stepped off a cattle ranch in Montana.

The three of us set off en route for the Taj Mahal. We spent a day getting to Jhansi and then waited for a train into Agra. After tipping a porter we were shown into a long, empty goods carriage where we staked out an area on the storage rack to sleep. Both Americans were amazed to learn that I slept on anything. I did not have any type of sleeping bag or even an under-blanket. Nor did I have any covering other than my increasingly soiled old camel coat.

But it was me who was more impressed by their toughness. Both men had served in Vietnam and had seen the most awful atrocities. They vividly described the use of flamethrowers which had the capacity to incinerate everything and everybody at whom they were directed.

Arriving in Agra at 3.30 A.M. there was a full moon and having been told by a horse-drawn tonga driver that these were the best conditions under which to see the Taj Mahal we set straight off. It was numbingly cold but the three of us were in good spirits during the 25 minute journey. We paid the driver, who having turned his horse around and was starting to trot off, shouted over his shoulder, 'Opens at six-thirty.'

We wandered around trying the enormous doors and peering up at the gigantic wall. I was keen to experience Taj Mahal by moonlight as had been suggested and wanted to get in by any means possible. Rightly the two Peace Corps workers said they were informally representing their country. Under those circumstances gaining entry to the Taj Mahal by breaking and entering did seem inappropriate.

Walking around did not alleviate the cold which we felt more and more intensely. We passed numerous small groups of people sleeping in doorways, huddled together like piglets for warmth.

Eventually we came across a small chai shop which was just opening. By this time we had walked throughout many of the mediaeval streets down to the banks of the Jumna river from which we had a view of the minarets rising eerily out of the early-morning mist.

The teahouse proprietor picked up a couple of lumps of dried buffalo dung, broke them with his dirty hands and started a small fire. To my consternation he handled all of our chapattis with the same unhygienic hands. Clayton said I should not worry about this, and passing the pepper joked:

'Sometimes they even put powdered dung into the pepper to make it go further. But,' he went on, 'the real problem is that none of the dung gets returned to the land where it is really needed as fertiliser.'

As if to confirm this point we witnessed an incident involving two dung-collectors, known euphemistically as sweepers. Harijans or Dalits survive at the bottom of the already painfully stratifying Indian caste system. Pathetically, these two "Untouchables" were in a heated debate over who had the right to collect a steaming deposit recently delivered by one of the ubiquitous, wandering cows.

Still seriously cold, the three of us returned to the Taj Mahal and were the first to be admitted. It was awe-inspiringly beautiful as the rising sun cast its orange light and low shadows over the white marble.

After covering our feet with the woollen slippers provided, we went inside to inspect intricate carving and inlay work around the tombs of Shah Jahan and his wife Mumtaz, for whom the mausoleum had been built.

Our guide unintentionally made us laugh by referring to the Taj Mahal as 'The most beautiful erection of a man for his woman'.

We toured Agra's Red Fort and stood on the balcony, where after imprisonment by his son, Shah Jahan spent the remainder of his life looking down at the Taj Mahal. We were told that he had planned to build an identical Mahal out of black marble on the other side of the river to be used as his own mausoleum.

My first reaction was to regret that the second building had never been constructed. After giving the subject more thought I considered things to be right the way they were.

A second structure, especially one built of black marble, would perhaps have been a distraction from something which was already as near perfection as is possible. What the Indian poet Rabindranath Tagore had described as, 'A Teardrop on the Cheek of Time.'

Walking back to the station a tri-shaw passed, aboard which I was delighted to see Ron. But he had not been visiting cultural sites such as the Taj or the Red Fort. Instead he had been busy selling his range of cheap, counterfeit watches.

My already fair hair had been increasingly bleached by the sun. It was also long, especially in comparison to the Americans whose hair, though not crew-cut, was short. So with time to spare at the railway station I too, had my hair cut.

In New Delhi I was taken by Clayton and Clive to the American Peace Corps hostel. It felt wonderfully indulgent, not only have a bath but to be able to laze in this large marble structure dating back to the days of the Raj. Much to my regret I was not able to stay in the Peace Corps hostel beyond the first night. Taking pity on me, Clayton gave me a lovely warm Peace Corps blanket as a farewell present.

Immediately opposite the Peace Corps hostel a small crowd had gathered. As usual, it was a noisy and chaotic group, who on this occasion were trying to put out a modest fire. They were throwing buckets of water regardless of the fact that the flames were coming from an electrical box. Common sense was the first casualty of any group activity in India.

The Sikh religion requires their temples to offer food and lodging to travellers, so making these places popular among the backpacking fraternity. On arrival I was shown into a small dark room containing several rucksacks spread over a raised but very dirty floor.

Laying my things down in a corner I tried to spruce myself up as much as possible in preparation for a visit to the British food company's New Delhi office. This was now managed by Roddy, with whom I had briefly overlapped in head office.

He was about four years older than me and had come through the same management training programme - and like me, won his spurs 'on the road.' His apparent confidence belied many of the insecurities from which I had also suffered. The difference was that he was an unabashed self-promoter.

I was disappointed to learn that my old friend, or should I be more honest and say someone who had considered me to be a potential rival, was away from Delhi on a business trip. Or was he? My sixth sense told me he was in the office and could possibly even hear my interaction with the receptionist.

But for some reason, he did not wish to meet with me, let alone feel any obligation to do anything for me. A game of one-upmanship perhaps, which was definitely his modus operandi. Or had he been speaking to

221

Benedict and now considered me a lost cause with whom he could not be bothered. None of that mattered when, as I was leaving the receptionist called out,

'Oh, there is a letter here for you. It's from New York.' It was so welcome, so beautiful and so loving.

'Hi sweetheart,

Paul that was the most wonderful letter you sent me. You put into words so beautifully what you want to say. I wish I could do the same. You are the only person I know that I feel that I'm on the same wavelength in feeling about things.

I hope we can find a solution and want to be very close to you. I too hope that we will always add to the fulfilment and enjoyment of our relationship and not stand in the others way. You have such a marvellous loving and understanding nature which are the traits I love about you. I think as you grow older you will turn into such a wise person.'

After a couple more pages of trivia the letter concluded.

'Thursday was Yvette's birthday and at the last moment Frank and I decided to give her a party. So on Wednesday night we called about 10 people and asked them over for dinner.

Both Ray and Jimmy came to the party. We had pretty good entertainment for Ray sang, Jimmy played the bongos and Frank the guitar. Everyone asked about you and Ray did an imitation of you answering the phone with 'Paul He-ar.'

I am thinking of you Sweetie. it seems like so long and yet you are always in my thoughts.

Love and kisses Dagmar xxx

PS Freddie says an FBI special agent came to the apartment making enquiries and referring to you as a fugitive from justice!'

Oh shit! - I thought. The FBI! It came as no surprise that enquiries were being made, but I assumed it would be the NYPD that would send someone round to knock on the door. Not the heavy guns of the scary sounding FBI.

Staying in the same room at the Sikh temple were two Americans, as well as a Swiss boy - and Ron. Next door among others, was an English couple who could at best be described as unconventional. Both wore their hair shoulder-length and adding to their eccentricity were always accompanied by their pet macaque.

Local men would come to the temple every day to see if the travellers had anything to sell. Students from affluent Indian families wanted to buy any clothing that had an American label.

One morning, seven rather angry youths arrived asking for someone called "Scotty." Apparently he had cheated them out of a small amount of money. I genuinely did not know Scotty and unsurprisingly, none of the others admitted to any knowledge of him either.

One of the tenets of the Sikh faith is the langar, a meal provided free of charge to all visitors. Although this food was available every day it was so unpalatable, possibly deliberately, that we all ate at an inexpensive European restaurant on Connaught Circus. Sometimes we would see the odd English couple hanging around scavenging and waiting to be given any left-over food.

One of the Americans with whom I was sharing the room not only had appalling manners but was outrageously rude in all his dealings with Indians. I had no desire to take up his offer to visit the crowded narrow streets of Delhi's infamous red light district. Gawping at other people's misery seemed so totally inappropriate.

That night I became ill, suffering from both laryngitis and an upset stomach. My illness, combined with the fact that it was Christmas Eve, were determining factors for me to move from the Sikh temple into the YMCA, despite the relatively exorbitant cost of 10 rupees per night.

Also staying at the "Y" was Dr Fenton whom I had originally met in Hong Kong. He gave me the name of an antibiotic, but no actual prescription. So, with virtually no voice I had to badger a pharmacist until he finally agreed to sell me the medicine. Feeling as if I was at death's door I made my bed, took the pills and slept.

Christmas Day led me to reflect about a number of things. This was the first Christmas spent on my own in a distant, non-Christian country and without any family or friends. Every past Christmas had its established routines, some happy and joyful, others just boring.

For my father, this was probably the busiest day of his year. Christmas in a rectory has additional significance, and yet also disrupts the relaxed format enjoyed by most families.

The candle-lit midnight service was important and enjoyable. As dictated by tradition, an unaccompanied solo chorister would sing the first verse of "Once in Royal David's City." Then the choir would undertake a long procession from the vestry round the outer aisles and finally up the nave to the altar. My brother and I were always 'Cope Bearers' to our father for whom this must have been a proud moment.

This was the one service every year in which our church (and others across the country) was full to capacity. The timing of the service was also such that it coincided with closing time for pubs. So another annual tradition was the disruption caused by drunks in pursuit of a different spiritual experience.

The church itself was set in the centre of a large, centuries-old graveyard through which there was an unlit public footpath. One year, prior to my involvement in the midnight service I needed a pee and headed outside for this purpose.

An overweight, somewhat elderly man reeking of alcoholic Christmas cheer staggered down the footpath. Catching sight of my moonlit figure dressed in cassock and white surplus moving furtively among the tombstones, he let out a shriek before fleeing back in the direction from whence he had come.

As there were more services on Christmas morning we did not eat our special lunch until quite late in the day. This was particularly frustrating for children, as no presents would be opened until after this meal.

What I thought about and remembered with affection were the traditions and patterns of Christmas. The uplifting carols and annual attendance at Exeter cathedral for an inspirational performance of the Messiah.

The beautiful tenor air "Ev'ry Valley," containing the line, "The crooked shall be made straight." Was I trying to straighten out the kinks and oddities of my personality?

Dwelling on Handel's beautiful music led me to think about the two other religious choral pieces which always moved me so deeply. Mozart's Coronation Mass and Brahms' German Requiem. I might have lost whatever faith I once had but if nothing else had gained an appreciation for soul-enriching music and awe-inspiring architecture.

Yes, of course I was aware of the Christmas story,

but by this stage of my life, that is exactly what I felt it was. A lovely story with some historical foundations about a truly remarkable man.

From about the age of twelve onwards I had become increasingly sceptical. In a post-Darwinian world dictated by logic, the questions I asked were never answered to my satisfaction. Vague, elliptical responses allowed me to drift away from childhood belief through agnosticism into full atheism.

My Christian upbringing had left me in limbo, with a strong sense of right and wrong which might be morally desirable but not always useful in real life. Turning the other cheek was hardly a formula for success: and then there was the guilt. I could feel guilty about virtually everything.

In the film "Rebel Without a Cause," Marlon Brando is asked what he's rebelling against, to which he replies, 'What have you got?' If asked what I felt guilty about I could equally have responded, 'What have you got?'

The actress Joan Collins said, 'I've never felt guilt or jealousy. Those are two emotions I don't really understand.' How nice to be free of debilitating emotions: yet I do not understand how anyone can live a normal life without the self-control of conscience.

Rock-solid, unshakeable religious faith seemed to be both highly desirable and infinitely pitiable. How wonderful to believe we only had to follow a prescribed path to a glorious eternity and how terrible to be so blinkered that we questioned nothing.

Seeking a semblance of tradition and feeling alone, I attended Evensong at the Anglican cathedral. The entire congregation did not exceed ten people, none of whom spoke to me and it did nothing to raise my spirits.

226

On Boxing Day I returned to the European restaurant on Connaught Circus. I had been on the lookout for the Victoria Institute group whom I knew to be in New Delhi and was overjoyed to find them there.

Most of the girls seemed equally excited to see me but were quick to laugh at my rasping voice and wagged their fingers in disapproval at my short hair. Indeed, it did seem as if Samson-like, I had now lost something.

This time the group was un-chaperoned and I could have sat next to the Chinese girl with whom I had talked so much on the ship. But, I could see from her body language that she withdrew and a couple of the other girls squeezed in protectively on either side of her. She did not smile as I would have expected and I could not interpret her reaction.

My school days had taught me that whatever the reality of our teenage infatuations, we complicate and confuse them. To save face and protect ourselves we distort and rearrange the facts to comply with what is expected of us by those with whom we share our secrets. In doing so we sometimes sabotage that which we actually want most.

Later, I was to learn that Ron and the American had been thrown out of the Sikh temple by the police after they had beaten up a taxi driver. At a subsequent meeting with Ron I asked him to change some money: something I had done for him when he was in need on board the ship. Despite Ron's requirement for dollars he was only willing to offer me a lower rate than I could get on the street.

An argument ensued and Ron started to threaten me. I knew I would have been no match for him in a fight. He was a former labourer and had developed a strong upper body. Despite having instigated the aggression, Ron appeared nervous saying, 'I'm not afraid of you' which immediately signalled to me that he was.

I had always taken my height for granted. Not fully aware it had the potential to impress and even deter potential pugilists, especially those built closer to the ground. The outcome was we walked away in opposite directions never to encounter each other again.

After investing in long underwear, woollen gloves and a balaclava, referred to by the locals as a monkey hat, I visited the nearby money-changers. Then packing my pride and joy, the fine woollen Peace Corps blanket Clayton had given me, I set off for the railway station. Utilising my doctored student card, I purchased a discounted, third class ticket to Amritsar.

Chapter 17

THE HOMEWARD STRETCH

Having crossed the border into Pakistan I spent the night sleeping in Lahore railway station. In search of Pakistani rupees I once again set out to find money-changers. The notes I received were so fresh and clean I examined them suspiciously, trying to determine if the currency changers had bypassed the Pakistani central bank and undertaken their own printing.

Two idiot railway officials latched on to me saying that they were going to visit England. They really thought that just because I was English I would be able to secure British passports for them. Ingratiating themselves to me they provided tea and cakes, which in turn were repaid with polite conversation.

I was trying to get to Quetta as quickly as possible because it was there that I had arranged to meet a BBC writer and his companion. They in turn said they would take me across the desert to Zahedan in their VW camper.

Less than 20 years prior to this, both West and East Pakistan had been a part of India. Ethnically the people looked the same but the fact that this was a Muslim country was apparent. I relished the beautiful and frequent muezzin's song-like call to prayer spreading out from the minarets like ripples in a pond.

Also starting to admire and appreciate Pakistani self-control and self-imposed discipline which seemed lacking in Hindu India.

It was not long before the chaos and crowding started once again. There were so many people packed tightly in the train it was impossible to adjust my legs. Everyone was constantly on the move: a woman with numerous small children uninhibitedly slumped across my feet. One of the children had a stream of wax flowing from one ear, its congealed state indicating that it had been there for some time without any attempt at removal.

During this 24-hour journey the locals let me have a sleeper so at least I could stretch out my legs. Bombarding me with questions and constantly requesting photographs of my family, most people generously showed respect.

The train crossed the Indus river before moving slowly through numerous passes and tunnels. In the morning, panoramic views of mountains and valleys opened up as we approached Quetta.

Two of the men sitting opposite me were anxious to connect and insisted I smoke one of their Pakistani cheroots. As the carriage was already filled with a cloud of blue smoke I had no objection and joined them.

On arrival the two brothers were determined that I should have breakfast at their house. This was a typical Pakistani mud-brick, mid-terrace structure which they rented for 23 rupees a month. It had a front room which they never used, and a main room with two beds. This room also contained a small, iron fire-enclosure over which they cooked.

At the back there was a tiny, cupboard-like room in which they kept their food. Outside there was a compact yard and a lavatory containing earth-filled pans. These were removed and emptied as required just like the pre-Victorian British concept of 'night-soil.' The brothers insisted I should stay with them and like a prize animal, proudly showed me off to all their neighbours. One of their friends was a dentist in whose shop were rows of rusty, antiquated dental instruments and faded wall charts of teeth. The dental chair was at the back of the shop illuminated only by a solitary, low-wattage bulb hanging forlornly from a well worn, cloth-covered cable.

That night, as if watching television, the brothers stared at me while I sat on the floor, washing in a bowl of water. In front of me and without asking, the two men opened my wash-bag and carefully examined each object.

Taking out my Gillette safety-razor they twisted the handle to open its butterfly wings and reveal the iridescent blue blade. Their fiddling with my things was annoying but I knew that they meant no offence.

The brothers' neighbour repeatedly raised the subject of my religious beliefs and talked about Islam. This irritated me because I did not want anyone telling me what I should believe or how I should live. Later I came to realise that the neighbour was only doing what was required of him within his religion. That was to spread his faith and proselytise, yet the manner of his advocacy was annoying.

We attended a film show in a covered part of the bazaar. The plot was so painfully obvious and simple that language was no barrier. Then one of the brothers confided that he was engaged in an ongoing, illicit love affair.

He told how he and his beloved were able to pass letters to each other. On only one occasion had he been able to lift the girl's veil to snatch a daring kiss. Both brothers pressed me for information about what they believed to be the loose and immoral ways of Europe and America.

The meals they prepared were crude and spicy. One morning having dropped a blob of ghee butter on the floor he scraped up the dirt-encrusted stuff, placed it on a stale chapatti and handed it to me. Feeling I had learned enough about how the locals lived, I moved into the Dak bungalow.

Dak bungalows or guesthouses were to be found right across the Indian subcontinent. They provided simple accommodation and were originally built as rest houses along trade and mail routes. The basic concept was similar to coaching inns in England or staging posts in America.

The two rooms of the Dak bungalow filled quickly on that day with an assortment of people travelling eastwards. Among them was an English chap with a moronic girlfriend.

It was she who had said, 'I left my last boyfriend because he developed prostate cancer and I did not wish to catch it.' Nevertheless, it was a luxury for a traveller to have the company of any woman in that part of the world.

As it was New Year's Eve the group planned to hold a party and set off in search of liquor. A heavy-set Australian turned up in a battered car crudely painted with maps and kangaroos, boasting he could arrange anything from girls to ganja. The conversation that night was even more single-track than it had been in the Sikh temple. Student cards were modified to suit their new owner: currency was bought and sold.

Earnest discussions teased out details of various issues important to such travellers. How to negotiate customs, including the fact that men and women were searched differently. Rucksacks and shoes with hidden compartments and how to obtain phony currency receipts were discussed.

How, as a foreigner, to acquire a legal liquor licence in dry states and then purchase whiskey to be resold for profit, cashing in rupees or buying a passage with them. Where to sell your blood for the highest price. More preposterously, the topic was raised of selling cars in Nepal, or forging travellers cheques.

After the sun went down it was bitingly cold but our group had prepared by purchasing a load of firewood. Then someone unpacked a few bottles of what looked like fluorescent-orange paint-stripper. 'Whisky,' he announced proudly.

Having heard stories of such home-made concoctions causing blindness and liver damage I did mention this fact to the others. As this did not impress them I upped the ante, saying: 'Sometimes homemade liquor has been known to have an even more debilitating side-effect commonly referred to as death.'

As they took no notice I myself merely pretended to sip from a glass. Counterbalancing this one man downed an entire bottle on his own. Later in the evening, the fat Aussie turned up with two very drunk Pakistanis, one of whom had reason to be sad. He had purchased a second wife just prior to a law having been passed forbidding multiple marriage.

The other Pakistani, who was called something like Jarru, was supposed to be the local expert on all things illegal. Yet he had nothing to commend him other than a few pellets of hash. While fat Aussie was demonstrating the art of making reefers by heating the hash and squeezing tobacco out of cigarettes, Jarru dragged himself to the door intending to drive away.

Seeing that the man could barely stand, I went after him and switched off the ignition. This happened about four times until I became tired of repeatedly going into the cold. In the end Jarru drove off and I'm glad to say the following day there were no reports he had hit anybody or anything.

The English chap with the dumb girlfriend was called Kevin. He obviously thought himself as tough, worldly and street-smart. One of his typical bullshit comments was. 'I always sleep with a woman in my bed and a pistol under my pillow.'

That evening sitting around the fire he did pull out a small automatic pistol. Ensuring he had everyone's attention he ejected the clip, removed three or four rounds and made a gesture as if he was throwing them into the fire. I and everyone else dived for cover expecting the bullets to go flying. This of course was exactly the reaction Kevin had hoped for.

It turned out that the pistol was a gas gun which could shoot debilitating but non-lethal tear gas. Impressive and very useful I thought, deciding that one day I would get one for self-defence.

Three other men who had clearly been partaking of both the orange paint-stripper and the enhanced cigarettes were busy holding a knife-throwing competition. Tiring of this they decided to go in search of the local whorehouse. Given that they returned quickly the assumption was that they could not find such an establishment. Probably for the very good reason that in all likelihood there wasn't one in Quetta. Certainly not one that would be easy to find and available to foreigners.

The communal lavatory used by all guests at the Dak bungalow consisted of a small bridge built over a stream. Planks were missing in a couple of areas, allowing those who were sufficiently agile to squat comfortably despite being in full view of the wider world. Everyone was waiting to see who would be the first to topple off and fall into the stream.

Towards the end of the party I noticed one of the small outbuildings was looking even more dilapidated than I remembered. 'Oh yes,' said fat Aussie, 'that has been helping to keep us warm tonight.'

There were not enough beds in the bungalow for the number of people staying and I knew I would have to share a coir-rope charpoy bed with someone. Hoping it would not be fat Aussie I was relieved when a semi-sober Swede came over and flopped down.

When not showing off, Kevin interested me because of his lifestyle. Every summer he would rent a small harbour-front shop in Fowey, Cornwall. From this they sold hot Cornish pasties, chips and tea. Nothing complicated he said, simple food which holidaymakers wanted and on which there was a good mark-up. 'We make enough money to do whatever we want for the rest of the year. Usually go somewhere warm,' he said.

That gave me the idea that at some stage in the future I too might like to run my own business. I would not have to be beholden to any employer and presumably the amount of money I made would depend on my efforts and business acumen, but, if Kevin could make it work, so could I.

Meeting up with the BBC journalist and his friend, we set off on the dusty journey across the desert. We were joined by a Dutch family consisting of the parents and four children. The idea was that travelling in this two-vehicle convoy would offer an element of security for both groups.

On the first night I slept with one of the Dutch boys in a small luggage trailer which looked something like a large coffin on wheels. It was not only uncomfortable but extremely cold. In the morning there was a heavy layer of frost lining the inside of the "coffin" lid. Breakfast that morning was very welcome and tasty but in terms of quantity, totally inadequate.

The two vehicles set off allowing a reasonable distance between them so the dust would settle before the second vehicle covered that stretch of ground.

Every yard of the road had wash-board ridges running from side to side. It looked much like an enlarged roll of corrugated cardboard flanked by featureless desert. On the third day the Dutch car broke down and it was necessary to remove the engine for repairs. There was the worrying possibility that our group might be stranded for over a week. Erecting a large tent gave us more space and made life easier although the nights remained very cold.

We had broken down in a narrow, lonely strip of land which juts westwards like a brittle shard of glass into Iran to its South and the Lashkar Gah region of Afghanistan to its North. Anything and anybody could simply disappear without trace in this dangerous, inhospitable region.

Heralded by a distant plume of dust we saw a vehicle travelling towards us. The mud-encrusted vehicle pulled over and out stepped a swarthy, Pashtun- Afghani man of about 40. A mass of long black curly hair tumbled out beneath his traditional pakol rolled hat. His abundant full-facial beard, body odour and shalwar kameez knee length dress and baggy trousers, all contributed to his menacing look.

Of more interest to me was the English woman travelling with him. She was much the same age as me, having just graduated in psychology from Durham University. She was not classically beautiful and would not have been described as pretty but I found her sensual and attractive. (That's what being in a desert does to a red-blooded young man.)

Her hair was cut short in a way that was practical in the desert but probably had more to do with making a statement about male expectations of women. Although slim and petite even her hippie-style over-sized, loose-fitting sweater failed to conceal her sensual figure.

Her lover studied each of us suspiciously with his intense, penetrating stare. As his eyes locked on to mine I felt he could see into deep into my soul sensing my needs and desires. I had to admit to myself that he exuded a raw, feral energy and grudgingly I understood why this young woman found him attractive.

Now she and her rugged lover were heading into the Afghan mountains, with no particular plan, and no thought as to how long she would live in Afghanistan. More significantly she appeared to have no exit strategy in case she was swallowed up in this wild country where women are mere chattels.

My fascination for this woman was triggered by a variety of thoughts and emotions. As well as finding her attractive I envied her having studied psychology at university. My guess was she would have been the first family member to have gone to university and I had nothing but admiration for a woman who could boldly take such risks. Nevertheless, there was a very real danger that once inside Afghanistan her life would become one of controlled servitude.

I could have looked after her in a kinder, safer way than the Afghani man. But that was exactly the point. She did not want someone like me, stereotypically boring middle-class. She wanted something edgy, exciting and different. Moreover, this liaison was probably the best possible way to piss off her father. But what a price she might have to pay for that!

The following night, while sleeping in the tent with the whole Dutch family, I had a very sexual dream. Waking with the early morning light I became conscious of the fact that I had been writhing around and groaning. It may have been pleasant for me but was not well received by the Dutch family. From then on I was relegated to sleeping alone in the baggage trailer.

Fortunately the Dutchman fixed the engine within the next two days. Anxious to head off it was still necessary to push-start the car. Everyone pushed for a few yards. Then another few yards. Finally after about half a mile the engine managed to keep going in a rough, hesitant way.

Despite being hunched down in the backseat I was constantly hitting my head on the low roof. Finally, arriving at the immigration and customs post on the Iranian border I had the opportunity to get out and uncoil.

As the weekly train was due to arrive in about two hours and could be seen making smoke on the distant horizon the customs officer did not want to deal with our two vehicles. He was puffing himself up and getting ready for the big moment when he could stop the train and display his authority. After much badgering he obviously decided it was easier to get rid of the smaller group and gave only the most cursory check before releasing us.

At the border our group was joined by an attractive, recently-married Swiss couple. Now technically in Iran but in reality in a no man's land between Pakistan and Iran and still ravenously hungry we drove on through the desert seeing only distant silhouettes of camel trains and the occasional date palm.

It seemed hardly possible, but here the roads were

even worse. Moreover it was dangerous to drive at night as it was not clear exactly where the road was. In one incident the vehicle shook badly and started to slide. We realised we had just driven through a small river. Probably the only one within a hundred mile radius which had perversely made its course over the road.

Cold and hungry we arrived after dark at the Iranian customs post. The officials were pleasant enough and said we could sleep in a couple of rooms furnished only with thick carpets. I shared a room with the Swiss couple who at least could keep each other warm after the small oil stove around which we had been huddling was removed.

There was no toilet or washroom, only a pit in the garden. I washed in a crude ornamental pond before wolfing down a breakfast of bread. It came from a large, round flat-loaf, blackened from the oven and gritty with embedded sand.

Deciding that I had used, possibly abused, the hospitality of the BBC journalist sufficiently, I decided to leave the group and take the bus to Isfahan. This taught me two things. First of all I was still in a part of the world where some kind of unspecified remuneration was required in order to facilitate even the most basic transaction. Secondly, the Iranians I met seemed to be more interested in telling me what they thought I wanted to hear than facts.

For example, when I wanted an express bus I was told that was what I was boarding, despite the fact it proceeded to stop every two miles. So wary did I become that when the bus stopped for the night, I refused to get off and ended up sleeping on the back seat despite the bitter cold.

In the morning I went out early to get breakfast and

found the weirdest place; a dark, ancient cellar with a lunatic woman and an English-speaking boy. As had happened before, hunger outweighed my concerns about hygiene and I gulped down fatty broth and blackened bread washing them down with sweet tea.

The bus not only had a driver but also an assistant who sat ape-like on the engine housing sycophantically laughing at the driver's jokes. The only time he moved from this perch was when it was necessary to either remove or replace cardboard from the front of the radiator.

I soon learned that the best place to sit was just behind the driver because that is where my feet could keep warmest. About every half hour someone would chant a prayer and the remainder of the passengers joined in the responses. Prayers for our safety were entirely justified in a country where the only rule of the road was that the largest vehicle wins.

Our bus and an equally ancient rival tried to determine which was faster. Despite the fact that the corrugated, dusty road was only wide enough for one bus, they were within inches of each other juggling for position. The diesel engines roared like angry bull elephants while the tailpipes emitted Krakatoa-sized clouds of black smoke.

Given that we were in an empty desert, it would have looked pretty stupid to the next vehicle coming along to find two buses which had been travelling in the same direction, in a mangled heap surrounded by the dead and injured.

With hundreds of miles of desert behind me and an equal distance ahead, there were several occasions when a lone man could be seen just walking. There was nothing visible in any direction so the obvious questions were where had they come from, what were they doing and where were they going?

There were more sightings of distant camel trains, some of which turned out to be no more than a mirage. At night there was the occasional faint, flickering light which turned out to be somebody cycling across the crust-hard desert - not even cycling along the road.

On one bus a scruffy little policeman displaying his authority searched many of the passengers. For some reason I was never able to understand, the smuggling of socks was rife at this time. So after the policeman had checked numerous passengers for illicit socks he approached me with the loud demand, 'Passport.' He took the passport Iranian style, holding it upside down and pretending to read from the back page forwards loudly declaring in Farsi, that it was acceptable.

In Isfahan I shared a cheap hotel room with about three other people. I was never quite sure exactly how many as they constantly drifted in and out. No longer willing to pay for expensive film I was anxious to raise funds by selling the Praktika camera I had purchased in New York, I showed it to the others in the room. One man said he would like to buy it but as he had no money that was not an option.

According to my school atlas, the direct and therefore logical route for me to take was through the Iraqi capital Baghdad. Having been told that I would find it easier to sell my camera in Teheran, that is where I decided to go. This entailed catching another succession of buses, by which time I was used to the mud-hut tea-houses and the frequent calls to prayer.

Weekends were always a nuisance during my travels because they created delays in getting visas or transportation. At one time I was held up for three days when Jewish, Muslim and Christian holy days all fell in a row.

On two occasions when I had been taking photographs the locals became upset thinking I was obtaining photographs of their women. The only things that really interested me in this part of the world were the fabled Persian markets. Sometimes partially subterranean they reminded me of story book pictures of Ali Baba and the Forty Thieves.

The weather became increasingly inclement while I was in Tehran and I had difficulty selling the camera. After several days incurring the necessary living costs I finally managed to sell the camera to a photo shop. Even there I came within a hair's breadth of being cheated. It all boiled down to the use of language and numbers. I was to receive Iranian rials and was trying to calculate exchange rates. The effect was whether I would receive the equivalent of US $30 or US three dollars.

As soon as I had the money for the camera I rushed to the bus station in order to purchase a ticket to Baghdad, only to learn that the road had been closed by snow. Then it transpired that the hotel I was staying in had given my passport to the police despite the fact that I had a legitimate Savak clearance document.

Savak, although a nice, innocuous name sounding like a skin lotion was in reality, the brutal secret police force somewhat akin to the Stasi in East Germany. Many Iranians described Savak as the most hated and feared institution in the country.

So, the FBI was looking for me in New York and Savak were holding my passport in Tehran. All I needed now was the KGB and Mossad to take an interest in me.

It seemed I had wasted a lot of time and achieved very little. The attempt to cheat me in the camera shop left me feeling wary. The unnecessary removal of my passport was worrying and would at the very least, take time to retrieve.

The sunshine, warmth, and conviviality had come to an end. Now the journey had turned into hard work; I wasn't having fun anymore and if truth be told, my spirits were low.

Sitting in the bus terminal I was at a complete loss. After a while I exchanged a few words with a truck driver who was delivering carpets to Germany. I asked if I could travel with him. Communication was difficult because he spoke only Turkish and a little German. Finally, after just hanging around the police station until they wanted to be rid of me, I retrieved my passport and we set off in the truck at 8:30 P.M.

My happiness at leaving Tehran for my onward rush towards England was short-lived. Within ten minutes the truck driver stopped and went into a suburban house. I slept on the truck cab-bed and thought I had been abandoned until the driver reappeared at 11 A.M. the next day.

What a miserable journey lay ahead of us. My camel coat was no match for the freezing cold, especially during the process of putting on or removing chains. As if this wasn't bad enough it was the Muslim period of Ramadan and the driver did not eat between 5 A.M. and sunset. Consequently I also had very little to eat.

On one occasion when I purchased some dates and started to eat them everyone stared at me as the loathsome infidel they considered me to be.

The driver picked up various passengers, taking them a few miles and then charging them a modest sum. At the eastern Turkish border he picked up a young Iranian called Apos who much to my delight, spoke English.

The three of us spent the next 48 miserable hours travelling across Turkey. Not being able to speak directly to the driver it could be that he felt left out of the conversation. Whatever the reason, he became increasingly disgruntled and morose. So on reaching Ezurum in eastern Turkey, Apos and I decided to continue our journey by train.

Foolishly no fixed sum for travelling with the Turkish truck driver had been arranged. This led to lengthy and none too pleasant negotiations which ended with the driver receiving less than he felt was appropriate and I paying more than I considered to be fair.

We decided to take the train which was departing late that night. We bought food for the journey and Apos hired a horse drawn carriage to take us to the station. Ezurum is 2000 metres above sea level and at that time of year, very cold. The strong wind and deep snow made both of us feel as if we were in Siberia.

My student card did not impress the Turkish railway officials and both of us had to purchase full price tickets. Although we had obtained food for the journey we had not acquired any water.

Well before the age in which water was packed in plastic bottles we found this essential commodity was sold at an exorbitant rate on the train. The result was an ever increasing thirst and my thoughts being constantly of water, orange juice and beer.

From the train station on the Anatolian side of Istanbul I walked directly onto a ferry to cross the Bosporus. The late afternoon sun was low in the sky and though shining optimistically produced no discernible heat.

But then, like any rare and beautiful transcendent peak-experience, I was surprised and overjoyed by the mesmerising, surreal effect of ship's wake. A brilliant turquoise stream of foam effervesced for a 100 yards behind our vessel. This was neither a dream nor a hallucination: I was witnessing the most magical natural phenomenon. A vast bloom of plankton agitated into bioluminescence.

It was a miraculous sight on a far greater scale and substantially more impressive than the puny chemi-luminescence we had produced in flasks in New York.

The Danish-French geographer, Conrad Malte-Brun witnessing bioluminescence in 1849 described it as 'The light of the sea.' He went on to say that, 'It was a magnificent and imposing spectacle. Sometimes, the vessel while ploughing her way through, the billows appeared to mark out a furrow of fire.'

My spirits were lifted by this and the knowledge I was leaving Asia and entering Europe, my home continent. Istanbul, dominated by minarets, radiated its own unique charm and personality. Excitedly I sensed the hustle and bustle - the struggle between East and West. Two cultures in a perpetual tussle for supremacy.

Now I really started to feel I was close to home with the narrow cobbled streets winding through a magnificent display of Byzantine architecture. Everyone stepped briskly as if invigorated by the sea air. At the American YMCA my beard of 10 days was shaved off and I lingered long enough in a hot shower to feel civilised society might once again accept me.

Beautifully displayed oranges and easily peeled tangerines were abundant and inexpensive. They together with tursu, the local dish of chopped vegetables soaked in vinegar and white wine, nourished me physically and allowed me to regain my positive outlook on life. Sufficiently so to visit the Topkapi museum and take pleasure in learning about the strategic importance of ancient Constantinople.

The YMCA hostel was located in an old house which rambled upwards rather than outwards and my bed was at the very top. This was another meeting place for travellers, but since most of them were going eastwards they had not yet developed the informality and sense of fraternity, which in time becomes ingrained in the more experienced.

It was in the "Y" that I met two very strange characters. For travellers they were old, perhaps mid to late thirties. One - a short heavily bearded Scot, unimaginatively named Scotty, talked incessantly in his thick brogue about Scottish independence. His companion, a New Zealander, was weak and ineffectual giving the impression of a man who had never fitted in anywhere.

Another indication of their peculiarity was that both men had invested money in the purchase of numerous Meerschaum pipes. To whom they thought they would be able to sell these was never explained other than by the comment that 'lots of people would want them.'

The Scot owned a tired, dented Austin A30 which had already been worn-out through many years service as a British Post Office van. Then it had toured Europe with a couple of further owners. As Scotty was himself unable to drive, he had teamed up with Fred the New Zealander to drive across North Africa, through the Middle East and they were now on their homeward journey via Athens.

Athens sounded pretty good to me and I managed to persuade the others that an additional driver would make the journey easier for them. After delays caused at the Greek Embassy relating to the acquisition of visas, we finally managed to leave around midday.

Scotty curled up in the back of the van surrounded by junk and assorted petrol cans. When I was driving we managed to get the speed up to nearly 40 mph, much better than the 30 mph achieved by Fred. But the old A30 was a sad contrast to the sleek Pontiac Catalina and overall, progress was slow.

At about 10 P.M. we stopped in a small Greek village to eat, selecting the noisiest Taverna. It was filled with soldiers, all dancing with each other. They were friendly and there was the potential to have a lively evening. But the other two wanted to press on, and after driving around Thessaloniki in circles we eventually found the road heading northwards along the coast.

Passing one romantic moonlit bay after another we peered down at the villas stacked almost vertically as they tumbled down to the shore. There was so much beauty here I wondered if it had been necessary to travel around the world when this jewel was to be found so close to home.

After many more miles of beautiful scenery and two punctures in the patched inner-tubes, the A30 chugged into Athens in the late afternoon. Fred and Scotty smoked pipes most of the time, substantially reducing the level of oxygen available to all of us. On arrival in Athens we were all tired and thoroughly dishevelled, our clothes smelling of smoke, petrol and general neglect.

Obviously lost, an English girl advised us how to get to the YMCA. We took her to a coffee shop where she told us of her experiences in Athens. I got the impression that every girl in a strange city thinks that all men are pursuing them for a single purpose. Maybe it was true that local men everywhere did try to take advantage of foreign women as by now I had heard the same story from Singapore to Athens.

Finding the YMCA to be full, we were directed to a house known only as, "Lilly's." Climbing the dark stairs we noticed that the third floor was swarming with young, predominantly pretty and to use the vernacular of the time, very "hip chicks." Sadly we were relegated to the fourth floor which was populated by bearded, guitar-strumming young men.

Many of these sun-kissed, dope-smoking stoners appeared to have no thought of the future let alone that it might entail responsibility. These semi-permanent residents lolled about lethargically all day, referring to themselves as students or artists.

In reality they were a torpid bunch who merely squandered the abundant freedom provided by affluent parents. If only those indulgent fathers and mothers were aware of the indolent lifestyle their money was buying, or how many abortions were they unknowingly funding?

Or perhaps subconsciously they did know but were themselves living vicariously through their offspring, enjoying a freedom and lifestyle which family circumstances and the war had denied them. The whole scene appeared to be fun at first, but the artifice of loucheness was superficial and I quickly tired of it.

The owner of the establishment, Lilly, was an amazing old girl who spoke several languages and charged very little for the beds. At night, because she was almost blind, she felt each bed to check if the occupant was safely accounted for. Fortunately I had been forewarned about this practice and so her soft touch sometime after midnight came as no surprise.

Food was not expensive in Greece and it was there I acquired a love of real yoghurt; thick creamy stuff with a leathery skin on top. After having a good look round Athens, including a visit to the Acropolis, the three of us purchased visas to enter Yugoslavia.

I also purchased a rail ticket which would take me from Athens to London. The very fact that this ticket had

London written on it made me happy. After spending a year during which I was always a foreigner and particularly since my recent experiences, I wanted to re-immerse myself in the customs and lifestyle which came naturally to me.

This in turn brought the realisation that it was not England from which I had wanted to escape, it was the circumstances of my life. The restrictions which had been imposed on me by my parents and society in general, were purely arbitrary. I no longer had to be bound by such shackles.

Boarding the train at about 9 P.M. I hastily found my corner seat. The coach filled rapidly until there were people lining the corridors. With a two and a half day rail journey ahead of me, I was pleased to learn that the seats slipped down together to make one long bed. This of course would have to be shared by two people, and once again my height ensured that I would not be able to lie straight. Moreover, with eight people lying sardine-like within each other's contours, none were able to turn over unless the entire group did so.

Many of the Greeks were travelling to work in Germany. One man in the carriage had a portable record player and a load of Greek records. The endless bouzouki music had a sameness about it but did liven up the journey.

My first attempt to reach the lavatory was unsuccessful because the corridors were so packed that it was impossible to pass all the people and their luggage. At my second attempt I went in the other direction, not heeding the objections of all the passengers sitting on the floor or pressed against the sides.

I might not have understood what they were saying

but clearly I had broken some kind of unwritten rule about moving through the carriage. At last reaching the lavatory I opened the door only to find it stacked from floor to ceiling with suitcases.

After the passengers had all sitting cross-legged for half an hour, the train stopped in the middle of nowhere. People poured out of every carriage into the bushes regardless of how long the train might remain there. Once back onboard there was a palpable sense of relief.

Everyone in the carriage shared food and I ate their watery cheese and grilled fish as well as olives and other Mediterranean specialties. On one occasion when I asked for water I was apologetically told there was only wine left. Such good wine! Embracing the warm and generous hospitality known as xenia, I felt as if I had Greek blood flowing through my veins.

After travelling through the recently earthquake stricken Skopje I once again fought my way over the suitcases towards a toilet. A few feet from my destination I was told in no uncertain terms to return to my carriage. Those people travelling in the corridor were tired of the constant aggravation of people stepping over them to get to the lavatory.

In no mood to be browbeaten by selfish people I refused to go back. When I glanced behind me there was a line of women also wanting the lavatory. So I was now negotiating not merely for myself but for others as well. Negotiating sounds pleasantly civilised and diplomatic for what in reality was a fairly heated argument.

As opponents we were in no danger of coming to blows as there was insufficient space for anyone to take a swing. Finally I agreed to their 'face-saving' demand that I would not waste time by shaving, which of course I had never intended to do. In return for this concession the women would also be allowed to pass. Travelling through the Alps I was awe-struck by the breathtakingly beautiful scenery. Emerging from each winding tunnel we were presented with yet another vista, yet another snow-laden mountain.

Austria seemed so generously endowed with beauty I felt an urge to get off the train and simply engage with nature at her best.

The train arrived in Cologne at 7:30 P.M. on Saturday night, after having left Athens on Thursday. It was freezing cold and my connecting train was not due to depart until twenty minutes past midnight. There were no restaurants open and no waiting rooms.

Desperately hungry I eventually obtained the correct one Deutschmark coin for a vending machine. Inserting the coin, my hands were so cold and numb that they slipped on the smooth handle allowing the heavily sprung compartment to slam shut. So I had lost my carefully acquired coin and remained hungry.

Throughout my travels I never had a sleeping bag. There were certainly sleeping bags at the time but they were all too bulky and heavy to be carried around. Moreover, backpacks as we know them today with their lightweight frames and comfortable straps had not been invented. The closest things available were ex-army Canvas packs.

So wrapped in my blanket, wearing my brown balaclava and woollen gloves I curled up shivering on the platform bench and tried to rest. But my feet hurt so much from the cold, sleep would not come.

What a strange sight I must have appeared using my battered old rucksack as a pillow. By 12 o'clock the train was still not on the platform and I made appropriate enquiries. Annoyingly I learnt the train had been parked on another platform and that I could have boarded sometime ago. As soon as I did get onto the train it moved to the platform on which I had been sitting for so long.

The eight hour train journey to Ostend passed quickly and then after a mere ferry ride I was back in England.

THE EPILOGUE

It was sheer joy to sense the familiarity of Dover's crumbling Victorian railway station with its humidly warm, mahogany-lined ticket office and damp, smelly lavatory. Home at last in England, drinking tea, eating bacon and eggs and reading an abandoned copy of the Sunday Express.

That paper included a column by the American agony-aunt Ann Landers. It said that, "when we are twenty we think everyone is looking at us; when we are 40 we do not care if anyone is looking at is; when we are 60 we realise that no one is looking at us."

That opened my eyes to my arrogant self-delusion that I was somehow at the centre of my world when in reality, life should be about looking outward rather than inward. Introspection can be useful but must be employed sensibly and in moderation.

In no time at all the Kent countryside melted away and I was in London. Familiar old florins, shillings and copper pennies weighed heavily in my pocket. Riding the underground and marvelling at English faces as if I had never seen them before; memories flooding back as if I had been away for a lifetime.

I knew exactly where my first port of call would be and longed to see my dear grandmother whom I knew would be overjoyed to have me back. I visualised the food she would rush out to get and how she would fuss over me.

While abroad I was always the foreigner. Now in my own country dressed in dirty trousers, draped in a soiled blanket and carrying a filthy back-pack, I still felt out of place. I had left England looking like a public schoolboy and now returned looking like a vagrant.

Coming into the railway station twenty miles west of London I caught sight of the food factory where I had worked until a year ago, immediately noting the familiar smell. The production lines would still be churning out the same products and in the offices; most of those familiar faces would still be sitting lethargically at the same desks. Their circumstances and outlook on life not substantially altered from when I last saw them.

A year ago I had saved £200. Now I returned with approximately the same amount but was so very much richer. New York had taught me how to make friends and have fun; I had been awe-struck by the Northern lights in the Yukon and mesmerised by bioluminescence on the Bosporus.

I had spent time laughing with a Buddhist monk and slept on the deck of a ship crossing the Bay of Bengal. I had received guidance and wisdom from two women, one Japanese and one Balinese. Most important of all, remembering dear Dagmar affectionately to this day, I had loved and been loved.

I had learnt to remember and acknowledge those wonderful people whose touch and connection had enriched my life. I had learnt the simple lesson that how someone speaks or which school they attended was irrelevant. The important thing was the character of the person; were they open to new ideas and experiences, and what did they contribute?

I walked the mile or so to 5 Castle Street, the shabby terraced house where my mother had grown up: the same house in which I had lived for over two years under the abominable pretence of being a mere lodger. Shame and class consciousness now seemed irrelevant, and throwing off my St Peter-like cloak of denial, I hugged Mrs. G, the one person who really cared about me.

'Oh Granny, how happy I am to see you,' I said.

Phoning my brother James, he suggested it would probably be alright if I came to stay with him for one or two nights. Recently married, he was employed by a heavy engineering firm in Birmingham. I had not expected to be greeted like the prodigal son but did anticipate a modicum of warmth.

As he had not experienced anything to cause change in his life, he retained the unexcitable, unemotional aloofness engendered by our upbringing. 'Good trip?' He enquired somewhat mechanically as if I had just popped out to the shops.

James had no interest in hearing about my travels and I struggled to work up enthusiasm for the engineering firm's Rugby club which was the centre of his social life. The only reference he made to our family was to imply having been let down by our parents who had selfishly gone off to live in Bermuda and in so doing scattered our already fractured little family.

We were brothers, who despite having apparently come out of the same mould, were very different people. Our interests and aspirations would inevitably take us on ever divergent paths.

Phoning the Nicholson home I was hoping to speak to Mrs. Nicholson. The doctor answered but after a few pleasantries gave me the shocking news that his wife had died four months ago. I was so sad to lose this boisterous outgoing woman. Perhaps, when she said she would never see me again it had more to do with her lung cancer than my likelihood of remaining in America.

The Shakespearean quotation she had written out prior to my departure, had given me much to think about during the past year. 'This above all: To thine own self be true, and it must follow, as the night the day, thou canst not then be false to any man. Farewell.'

My interpretation of this was the desirability to act with honesty for my own benefit and that of the rest of the world. To reveal my true self, not hide behind an image I wished to portray, or disappear chameleon-like into the crowd. By honesty it meant having worthwhile intentions and direct communication.

What a pity Mrs. Nicholson could not see me now. She would have been so encouraging and proud of her handsome torchbearer.

Dr Nicholson invited me to come and stay for a couple of days which I gladly accepted. It gave me the opportunity to visit a few people and make contact with school friends.

Meeting the latter in a lively Exeter pub, everyone was interested in seeing each other and especially hearing about Tom in Singapore. My schoolmates did find it remarkable I had been round the world but their interest was not in the architectural wonders of Isfahan but in the flesh-pots of Southeast Asia.

The oak-beamed Tudor inn in which we met was the same one we had all been in a few years earlier when I was with Claire. The time when everyone had been so envious of this beautiful young couple.

Claire was friendly enough when I phoned but was mainly interested in talking about her engagement to an army officer. This, she said disparagingly, meant that she would have to leave Seavale and might even have to go and live in Germany. 'How awful to be so far away from home.' she said.

Dr Nicholson contacted the local newspaper who interviewed me. The result was an enthusiastic article highlighting what a remarkable journey I had completed. The headline read 'Local Man Undertakes Great Odyssey - Circumnavigates globe and travels from Arctic to Equator.'

As with my school friends, the newspaper missed the point. The geographical expedition was merely a process which allowed the opportunity to experience and learn. Moreover, if they wished to refer to the Odyssey it would have been better to quote Ulysses when he said: 'I am a part of all that I have met' and to explain what he meant by that.

On my second and final afternoon with Dr Nicholson he suggested we should take the dog for a walk. This attractive, formerly ebullient man moved slowly, he had lost his spark and vitality. His guiding star, his cheerful, witty, and at times outrageous companion, was no longer by his side.

At the top of Highmount Hill we sat on a bench looking at the patterns formed by the sea. Knowing about my original idea of sailing across the Atlantic in a small boat, he said: 'There was an article in the paper about a Polish sailor and a young man who set out from Plymouth on a transatlantic voyage. The boat foundered in a storm west of the Scilly Isles. One of them was drowned, the other survived.'

He did not know, or refrained from telling me, which one had drowned and which survived. This news shattered me: it was upsetting in many ways. It could have been me in that ordeal and it could have been me who died at the age of twenty. Or if it was Powidsky who died that was also tragic: he appeared to be a decent and honourable man.

After sitting in silence for a while Dr. Nicholson said he had to return for evening surgery, and leaving me in contemplative mood, started to walk down the hill. The Labrador's loyalties were put to the test. Would he stay with me for the fun of having sticks thrown or return home where his dinner bowl would be waiting?

Tail wagging and choosing the latter, I realised that food trumps most things in life and that even dogs have to make decisions. What decisions did I now have to make? How could I earn my living and what job would I go into? Where would I live, indeed where did I wish to live? What did I want from life?

Understanding now that although well-meaning, my parents' narrow and restrictive views of the world did not have to be mine. I had escaped from that repression and could choose to believe in any God or none; I would find my own wellspring for inspiration and guidance. I did not have to be sexually debilitated by inappropriate and misguided guilt stemming from parental and prevailing social attitudes.

I came to the conclusion that all of us live in our own little sphere of self-serving thought and activity. Of course we care about other people but even this concern is interlinked with how those people affect us.

I recognised that there was a price to be paid for this. The fact that I could not hold on to a girlfriend was because I was constantly on the move and if truth be told, afraid of being pinned down; always wondering if there was something or someone better over the horizon.

If I could snap my fingers and re-set my past few years would I wish to be working locally and engaged to Claire or someone like her? If I could return to the United States, which at this time was impossible, would I wish to settle into middle-class American domesticity with Dagmar?

Thinking about this I recognised patterns of my behaviour which would either prescribe the rest of my life or needed to be amended.

I was in no doubt that my decision to abandon the United States rather than face military conscription had been the right one; yet aware that my departure could rightly be seen as an act of cowardice. But my experience during the Army medical examination in New York was enough to convince me I had no wish to go into the American army.

In any case it seemed like commonsense to avoid transportation to fight in terrible war in which I might have been psychologically damaged, physically maimed or even killed.

Affectionately, I thought of Dagmar, remembering her playfulness and laughter. I wanted that but I also wanted something more. I wanted to study psychology, to learn about other cultures, other traditions, other religions and philosophies. To study so that I too could take pleasure in the wisdom and articulacy of some people whom I had met on my journey.

The School of Oriental and African Studies would be ideal for me but without the qualifications to get into London University that was not possible. An alternative was Birkbeck College which was making it possible for people to take evening courses which would eventually lead to a degree.

Dr. Nicholson had asked what my plans were. He suggested I would be good at helping people find flats and houses and offered to refer me to a friend who ran a successful estate agency in London. That sounded interesting to me, something I would enjoy combined with life in London which surely could be as exciting as New York.

After all, this was 1965 and London was gaining a reputation for being the centre of growing social and sexual freedom.

The fashion scene was interesting as well. Away from the workplace, men had taken to wearing psychedelic shirts and flared trousers. Hemlines went higher and higher, finally resulting in the miniskirt. (Which some girls referred to as the helicopter skirt - because you could see into the cockpit.)

Mary Quant who was credited with this design said that 1960s girls were rebelling and wanted to be noticed, to feel sexy and to feel good.

The class system was slowly starting to erode. People like the model Twiggy and musicians like the Beatles showed it was talent not pedigree that counted. Grammar schools had opened the doors for bright people from working-class backgrounds to rise to the top in their chosen professions. Fortunately a more egalitarian society was emerging.

Never again would I confine myself to socialising with any particular group. America's open society had taught me to value the individual, not their background. Now I wanted to mix with bohemians, people in the arts, photographers, theatre people – any group in fact where human character was less constrained and more interesting.

I had gained so much from my experiences.

The ability to move from one situation to another, the confidence to socialise and make friends. Now believing in my ability to cope and having developed a useful level of resilience and fortitude.

An understanding that my failures and my modest successes were mostly the result of my decisions and my actions. The realisation that my destiny would be shaped not merely by circumstance and chance but by the responsibility I undertook for it.

At the age of 21 my life was still largely unwritten. How many pages that book would contain and what those blank sheets would reveal was still a mystery. That is what makes life both exciting and potentially terrifying.

We become the people we are through the accumulation of our experiences and the effect those experiences have on us. My journey had not been a rapid, let-alone complete metamorphosis. It had, however, initiated movement towards the level of understanding we call maturity.

My gaze no longer swept inattentively over Seavale's cliffs. Now I savoured the warmth and charm of their terracotta sandstone, noting how steeply they dropped down to the stony shoreline. These were my cliffs, those were my screeching seagulls; this was my home.

Walking back I understood the joy of diversity. The unassuming beauty of Seavale's bluebell woods were not to be compared with the flamboyant lotus ponds of Southeast Asia. People did not have to be compared and valued to a greater or lesser extent. It is enough to appreciate them - each individual for who they are.

Before leaving Seavale I made a nostalgic visit to the ancient church. The scroll showing former incumbents listed their names back to 1628, with my father's now second from the bottom.

My heart jumped with delight when I saw pinned to a notice board, a faded poem written in ink, in my father's handwriting. After reading it I felt that overcoming physical distance, this was a message of love and support directly from him to me. The poem written by an unknown author read,

To a Special Person.

People come into your life for a REASON, a SEASON or a LIFETIME. When you know which one it is, you will know exactly what to do.

When someone is in your life for a reason, it is usually to meet a need you have expressed outwardly or inwardly. They have come to assist you through a difficulty; to provide you with guidance and support; to aid you physically, emotionally or spiritually.
They may seem like a godsend - and they are.
They are there for the reason you need them to be. Then, without any wrongdoing on your part or at an inconvenient time, this person will say or do something to bring the relationship to an end.
Sometimes they die. Sometimes they walk away. Sometimes they act in a way that forces you to take a stand.
What we must realise is that our need has been met, our desire fulfilled. Their work is done. The prayer you sent up has been answered and now it is time to move on.

When people come into your life for a season, it is because your turn has come to share, grow or learn. They bring you an experience of peace or make you laugh. They may teach you something you have never done before.

They usually give you an unbelievable amount of joy. Believe it! It is real! But, only for a season.

Lifetime relationships teach you lifetime lessons; those things you must build upon in order to have a solid emotional foundation. Your job is to accept the lesson, the love, and the person.

To put what you have learned to use in all other relationships, and areas of your life. It is said that love is blind but friendship is seeing with understanding and compassion.

Thank you for being a part of my life.

That poem sparked the memory of a quotation which is as true today as when it was written in the 18th century. Alexander Chalmers said, 'The three great essentials of happiness are: Something to do, someone to love and something to hope for.'

I was starting to understand what the Danish philosopher Soren Kierkegaard meant when he said, 'Life can only be understood backwards; but it must be lived forwards.' And that, 'Life is not a problem to be solved, but a reality to be experienced.'

It was said of Ulysses that he was a perpetual guest. I too felt that I had been plucking fruit as I travelled but had given little back in return. Now was the time to reveal the person I had become and use my new found freedom to engage with, and give to others.

My experiences had been a catalyst for growth and change but I was by no means fully fledged. Yet I had proved to myself that even if I did not fly with the grace of a swallow, I could remain airborne. I could glide with optimism on the winds of my own choosing.

Had I invented the Gap Year? No of course not.

Ulysses did that two and a half thousand years ago. More recently Laurie Lee, Patrick Leigh Fermor and a host of other mavericks added their names to that worthy pantheon.

But I had invented MY Gap Year, and that was good enough for me.

ABOUT THE AUTHOR

A graduate of the University of Alberta, Paul W. King was born to British parents in Kashmir prior to partition.

For several years he was involved in taking oil and gas related trade missions from Canada to many South East Asian and Pacific countries. He has worked for large corporations, including the professional photography department of Kodak (Canada) Ltd, and Canadian government trade organisations, as well as spending twenty years in various business related posts in Europe.

He has spent a lifetime meeting and subconsciously studying scores of people in a variety of cultures. He attributes his interest in, and understanding of human nature to his own search for answers and the knowledge passed on to him by so many wise and fascinating people.

ACKNOWLEDGEMENTS

This is to acknowledge the tireless encouragement and support I have received from my wife Jeni in the writing of this book.

My gratitude goes to Mike George and Mike Olley for their input and suggestions. In particular I wish to thank the highly talented Jacq Molloy for her invaluable guidance.

And of course there are the many people, some of whom are recorded above, who have coloured and enriched the mosaic of my life.

Note. This memoir-style narrative is inspired by real events. Some aspects of the portrayal have been fictionalised or modified for dramatic purposes. The characters portrayed have also been fictionalised for storytelling effect and any resemblance between them and actual living individuals should not be inferred.